— THE —
FATHER
CONNECTION

— THE —
FATHER
CONNECTION

HOW YOU CAN MAKE THE DIFFERENCE IN
YOUR CHILD'S SELF-ESTEEM AND SENSE OF PURPOSE

JOSH McDOWELL

B&H
PUBLISHING GROUP

NASHVILLE, TENNESSEE

ISBN: 978-0-8054-4742-2
B&H Publishing Group
Nashville, Tennessee
www.BHPublishingGroup.com

Dewey Decimal Classification: 306.874
Subject Heading:
Father and Child / Christian Ethics / Fatherhood

Printed in the USA
10 11 12 13 14 15   17 16 15 14 13

TABLE OF CONTENTS

1. Being a Dad in Tough Times 1

2. The Father Connection 13

3. The Father's Unconditional Love and Acceptance 25

4. The Father's Purity 39

5. The Father's Truth 55

6. The Trustworthy Father 71

7. The Father Who Comforts and Supports 81

8. The Father as Refuge 93

9. The Father as Friend 109

10. The Father Who Disciplines 123

11. The Father and Forgiveness 141

12. The Father and Respect 153

13. A Father after God's Own Heart 165

60 Fun Things a Dad Can Do with His Kids 179

Endnotes 187

Acknowledgments 193

Dear Dad,

It is an honor and privilege to be writing you this letter. I am overwhelmed with appreciation for the way you love Mom, my siblings, and me. You always make me feel important. I cherish so many childhood memories of spending time together, such as playing with water balloons, jumping on beds, styling your hair, and going out for hot chocolate with ice cream in it. The way you consistently treated Mom with respect, spoke openly with me about sexual purity, and the "dates" you took me on as a teenager have imprinted on my mind how I want a man to treat me and has given me a healthy view of marriage. I pray that I will marry someone with your compassion and integrity.

I will be forever grateful for the way you demonstrated to me that my value comes from being created in the image of God. Knowing that I have inherent value helped me growing up to have the freedom to try new things and to fail without feeling like a failure. Thank you for giving me the tools to make right choices but loving me unconditionally when I make mistakes. You have modeled what it's like to admit mistakes and to seek forgiveness when needed, along with allowing others to make mistakes and being quick to forgive without resentment.

The time you spent with me while I was growing up showed me that you valued being my dad. The unconditional love you give me has allowed me to feel secure and be able to love others. I appreciate you so much and will always treasure the long talks and lots of laughter. You taught me to love God, care for others, and embrace life while living it to the fullest. I know this book will motivate other fathers to invest time in their kids and will give them the tools they need to empower their children to make right choices. I am so proud of you and grateful that you are my dad.

Love, Kelly

Dear Dad,

Even though I have heard you speak on parenting many times—and, of course, have been one of your personal subjects!—reading this book was a real eye-opener for me. Now that I am a dad, I find myself thinking, "How did my parents handle this? What would my dad do in this situation?" My heartfelt prayer is that God would enable me to be as good a father to my kids as you have been to Kelly, Katie, Heather, and me.

People often ask me what it's like to be the son of Josh McDowell. To the surprise of some, that's not the primary lens through which I see you—as your son. My first thought of you is as my father—the man who loves my mom, who sacrificed greatly to be at my basketball games, who overcame incredible challenges from his childhood, who said he was sorry when he was wrong, who laughs and enjoys life, and who boldly stands up for what he believes. For these reasons, I am proud to call you my dad.

One of the important points you give in this book is how critical it is to build memories with your kids. As I think back on my childhood, I am amazed at how many incredible memories you built for us as a family.

I remember many fun times, such as eating popcorn in the Jacuzzi, going on double dates, sleeping under a tarp in the rain in Kauai, and going to the Final Four. Yet I also remember when we brought a Christmas tree and some small gifts to Terry, since she had no family that cared for her. Seeing her cry and feeling the joy of giving will be forever etched in my memory.

You've had some amazing accomplishments in your life, Dad. But to me, the most impressive accomplishment is that you've been a father who truly connects with his kids. You don't just write about fathering. You live it. I love you!

Your best (male) friend,
Sean

Dear Dad,

I'll never forget the day you came to pick me up at my elementary school in a horse-drawn carriage to take my friends and me out for banana splits. I remember riding in the carriage through our small town, feeling unique and special. I have so many great memories of moments when you went out of your way to communicate your love and acceptance to me. I have always known that you love me and are proud of me.

I am often amazed at the way you relate with our family. Kelly, Sean, Heather and I have a far different relationship with you than you did with your father. In the first chapter of this book, you write:

"As a child, I never knew a father's love. I never benefited from a father's example. I can't remember a single time when my father took me somewhere alone and spent time with me. I can't remember feeling proud of my father, or imitating him."

It is painful for me to read those words because I know the deep hurt you have experienced as a result of your broken family, especially in your relationship with your father. But as I read these words I also rejoice. I rejoice in God's grace that he has shown me through you. It is because of this grace that I can say:

"As a child, I always knew a father's love. I consistently benefited from a father's example. I remember many times when my father took me somewhere alone and spent time with me. I am proud of my father, and I hope to imitate him in my parenting."

Dad, I am so thankful for the many times you went out of your way to communicate your love and acceptance to me. Your unconditional love for me has given me the freedom to live without fear of failure. I live each day knowing that I am loved and accepted, a blessing I do not take for granted.

I am so proud of you. I love you, and I love being your daughter.

Love, Katie

Dear Dad,

I've been thinking through our life together, and there are two very distinct things you have said to me over the years that have played a huge part in the amazing relationship we have as Daddy and daughter.

You once told me that I could sit in your lap "anytime, anywhere." At the age of nine, and now at the age of twenty-one, you have held onto and been faithful to that promise. But those many years ago, it was much more than reserved seating; it was the foundational promise that my dad would always be there for me "anytime," that no matter where he was, no matter who he was speaking to, he was my dad. While I'm sure you didn't expect me to be twenty-one and still needing to sit on my dad's lap, there is something in me that has always needed you. I love you so deeply, and I know that God intended you to be my dad long before I became a McDowell.

The second one is this: Do you remember when I was about thirteen, and I asked you what you would do if I got pregnant? At the time, I thought that this would be the most terrifying mistake I could ever make. But you responded so quickly and confidently. You said that you would love me no matter what happened, and that in any circumstance we would work it out together, because "that's what daddys are for."

Over the years, I have called you upset about school and boys, broken cars and papers, rental house issues and roommates, and with each call you have been eager to give wisdom and love to me . . . because that's what my daddy is for.

I love you so much and am thankful that God picked you to be my dad.

Love, Heather

CHAPTER 1
Being a Dad in Tough Times

More than thirty years ago, I held my firstborn child in my arms.

I vividly remember the thoughts and emotions that washed over me at that time. I looked down into the face of my newborn daughter, Kelly, wrapped in a soft yellow blanket. I counted her fingers and marvelled at the completeness and intricacy of her tiny form. She was helpless. She was priceless. And she was mine.

As I gazed at her in love and wonder, I felt another emotion rise in my breast, an emotion I recognized all too well. Terror.

"What am I doing?" I said to myself. "I don't know how to be a father!"

As a child, I never knew a father's love. I never benefited from a father's example. I can't remember a single time when my father took me somewhere alone and spent time with me. I can't remember feeling proud of my father or imitating him. In fact, I hated him. I grew up on a 150-acre dairy farm just outside a small town in Michigan. Everyone knew everyone else in that town and, of course, everyone knew about my father and his drinking. My teenage buddies made jokes about him, and I laughed, too, hoping my laughter would hide my pain.

I hated him for the shame he caused me, but also for the way he treated my mother. Sometimes I'd go out to the barn and find my mother lying in the manure behind the cows, beaten so badly she couldn't get up. Sometimes when he came home in a drunken stupor, I would drag him out to the barn, tie him to a stall, and leave him there to sleep it off. As a teenager, I would tie his feet with a noose that ended around his neck, hoping he would choke himself while trying to get free. When my mother died the month of my high school graduation, I blamed my father.

Though God generously brought about a reconciliation with my father after I became a Christian, and even allowed me to help him trust Christ for salvation (fourteen months before he died of a heart attack), I became a father with an acute sense of how unprepared I was to be a father.

The Most Frightening Job in the World

You may not have had such a poor relationship with your father, but you may share some of my realization that parenthood may be the scariest job in the world. To make matters worse, there's nowhere to obtain a license for fatherhood. There are very few job requirements. Most of us must learn on the job, by trial and error—mostly by error! In fact, someone has observed that most people don't really become good at being a parent until their *children* have become parents!

Over the years, I have observed and counseled many fellow strugglers—well-meaning dads who feel overwhelmed by the job of becoming an effective father. Many admit that they're fumbling in the juggling act of marriage, career, and fatherhood. Most feel trapped by their intense work schedules and the accompanying pressures. Many feel limited by a lack of practical fathering skills, by a difficult marriage, or by unhealthy patterns in their own lives.

Moreover, the challenges of fatherhood are even more pronounced today than ever before. We live in a world that often threatens our marriages, our families, and our children. We live in a culture that rejects the truth of the Bible, mocks biblical morality, glorifies sex and violence, and laughs at drunkenness and rudeness. We live in a society that has largely rejected the notions of truth and morality, a society that has somehow lost the ability to decide what is true and what is right, a society in which truth has become a matter of taste, and morality has been replaced by individual preference.

We are faced with the daunting task of raising children amid a culture in crisis. Research tells a statistical horror story of what is happening *every day* in America:

- 1,000 unwed teenage girls become mothers
- 1,106 teenage girls get abortions
- 4,219 teenagers contract a sexually transmitted disease
- 500 adolescents begin using drugs
- 1,000 adolescents begin drinking alcohol
- 135,000 kids bring a gun or other weapon to school
- 3,610 teens are assaulted; 80 are raped
- 2,200 teens drop out of high school
- 7 kids (ages 10–19) are murdered
- 7 juveniles (17 and under) are arrested for murder
- 6 teens commit suicide[1]

It is little wonder that many men face the task of fathering with fear and trembling. But fathering is not only in many respects the most *frightening* job in the world, it is also among the most critically *needed* jobs in the world.

The Most Important Job in the World

The task of being a father is of critical importance, and it has never been more so than in this day and age. A child's relationship with Dad is a decisive factor in that young man or woman's health, development, and happiness. Consider the following well-documented findings:

- Dr. Loren Moshen of the National Institute of Mental Health analyzed U.S. census figures and found the absence of a father to be a stronger factor than poverty in contributing to juvenile delinquency.
- A group of Yale behavioral scientists studied delinquency in forty-eight cultures around the world and found that crime rates were highest among adults who as children had been raised solely by women.
- Dr. Martin Deutsch found that the father's presence and conversation, especially at dinner time, stimulates a child to perform better at school.[2]
- A study of 1,337 medical doctors who graduated from Johns Hopkins University between 1948 and 1964 found that lack of closeness with parents was the common factor in hypertension, coronary heart disease, malignant tumors, mental illness, and suicide.[3]
- A study of thirty-nine teenage girls who were suffering from the anorexia nervosa eating disorder showed that thirty-six of them had one common denominator: the lack of a close relationship with their fathers.
- Johns Hopkins University researchers found that "young, white teenage girls living in fatherless families . . . were 60 percent more likely to have premarital intercourse than those living in two-parent homes."[4]
- Dr. Armand Nicholi's research found that an emotionally or physically absent father contributes to a child's (1) low motivation for achievement; (2) inability to defer immediate gratification for later rewards; (3) low self-esteem; and (4) susceptibility to group influence and to juvenile delinquency.[5]

Based on my interaction with hundreds of moms, dads, and kids, I would agree with those findings. Not only that, but the results of those studies correspond closely with research among youth in evangelical Christian churches as well.

Not too long ago, I commissioned a survey of more than 3,700 teens in evangelical churches—the most extensive survey of evangelical youth ever conducted. The research, assembled by The Barna Research Group, underscored the importance of the father connection with a child.

Of the 3,795 youth surveyed in that study, 82 percent of them attended an evangelical church weekly, and 86 percent said they had made a commitment to trust Christ as their Savior and Lord. Yet the study showed that 54 percent of teens and pre-teens in evangelical church families say they seldom or never talk with their father about their personal concerns (compared to 26 percent who say they seldom or never talk with Mom about such things). One in every four young people surveyed stated that they *never* have a meaningful conversation with their father. More than two in five (42%) say they seldom or never do something special with their father that involves "just the two of you." And one in five say their father seldom or never shows his love for them.[6]

At the same time, the study revealed that youth who are "very close" to their parents are:

- more likely to feel "very satisfied" with their life
- more likely to abstain from sexual intercourse
- more likely to adopt biblical standards of truth and morality
- more likely to attend church
- more likely to read their Bible consistently
- more likely to pray daily

The research—not only among Christian youth but among all young people—strongly indicates that the "Father Connection" is a crucial factor in a child's health, development, and happiness. This does not mean that mothers are not important. However, it does underscore the fact that in most cases, Mom has been there, doing her job, taking care of the children, talking to the children, and spending time with the children. As a result, it seems children have come to *expect* Mom to be accessible, loving, communicative, and accepting.

With Dad, however, the law of supply and demand comes into play. In many cases he is *less* accessible, *less* involved, or *less* communicative than Mom is. And because his attention and time are in shorter supply, an aura of greater significance builds around that relationship. Just like all of us, our kids crave what they do not have, and in too many cases they do not have a close relationship with their dads.

That is why the Father Connection is the most important factor in the life of your children, regardless of their ages. Dad, your relationship with your sons and daughters is a verifiably critical factor in their growth in wisdom, stature, and favor with God and man. You can make all the difference in your child's self-esteem, regard for others, and sense of purpose.

The Most Rewarding Job in the World

Although I began the experience of fatherhood with a less than perfect example in my own father, I have been blessed to know and learn from a series of models and mentors through the years. Chief among these has been my wife, Dottie, the most fantastic wife a man could ever have and a wise and loving mother to our four children. I have also learned much from Dick Day, who (next to my son Sean) is the closest male friend I've ever had. And Norm Wakefield, a friend with whom I've coauthored several books, has also been an example of an effective Christian father to me.

Norm and his wife, Winnie, are the parents of five children, all grown now. One of the most rewarding moments in Norm's life occurred when his son, Joel, was twenty-four.

"Joel's wedding was a special event for me," Norm says, "because he had asked me to be his best man. As I stood beside this young man, my mind flashed back many years. I remembered when Joel was a tiny preschooler and I was working on a doctoral program in Louisville, Kentucky. I arrived home one day to discover that my son had injured his head in a freak accident. I rushed Joel to the emergency room at the hospital. As the medical team began to do its evaluation, I was left alone with my fear and helplessness, and I began to sob as I realized how precious my son was to me and how I valued him." Before long, Norm learned that Joel's injury would not cause serious or lasting damage; he would soon recover fully. "But I discovered that day," Norm says, "how much my son meant to me."

For the next twenty years, Norm strived to be a loving, involved, and effective father to Joel and his four other children, an effort that seemed in many ways to culminate on Joel's wedding day. "As I stood beside that twenty-four-year-old son whom I love and respect," he says, "I was filled to overflowing with joy. I knew that he, like his sisters, was committed to honoring and serving Christ, and I knew he was committed to being a loving husband to Lisa, his bride. I was genuinely grateful for God's faithfulness. He had honored Winnie's and my commitment to love, enjoy, and nurture our children. In the process, they had become our dearest friends."

What a tribute Joel paid to his father! Of all the friends Joel might have chosen to be his best man—classmates, teammates, childhood playmates—he chose Dad!

Fatherhood may be the most frightening job in the world, but it is also the most important, most rewarding job any man can tackle. Regardless of your limitations or shortcomings, you can become an effective father. You can overcome the obstacles. You can counter the difficulties that are arrayed against you. You can become the father your children need.

I want to challenge, encourage, and motivate you to action by the ideas in this book. I don't pretend to be an expert at fatherhood. I had an inauspicious beginning. I have struggled often, perhaps in the same ways you have. I have failed many times. But I've learned much from others about being a dad, and I hope you'll be helped by those things that have been such a blessing to me in my relationships with my children.

I recognize, of course, that you may feel a bit uncomfortable as you read, realizing that you haven't been as effective as you could be. That's natural. We all experience the pressures of being a dad, and we can all improve somewhere. But I don't want you to fall into a guilt trap. See if these simple steps will help you avoid becoming consumed by regret and your own imperfections:

First, approach fathering from a positive, optimistic perspective. Look at fathering as a positive, loving influence that will not only enrich your child's life but also be a means that God will use to stretch you mentally, emotionally, and spiritually. Consider it an important opportunity to invest your life in someone, believing that the time invested will bear fruit for years—perhaps generations—to come.

Second, look at growth as a series of small steps taken over a lifetime. Don't allow yourself to be overwhelmed by what you aren't doing; rather, focus on some small, new step you'd like to take today. (At the end of each chapter are some suggested questions and action points to help you prioritize your ideas and move forward.) In no time, these little changes will make a significant difference in your relationships with your children. Also, keep in mind that no matter how hard we try, most of us will never feel completely satisfied with our parenting. So make a conscious effort to redirect this dissatisfaction into steps for growth instead of occasions to become discouraged or depressed.

Third, determine to dedicate yourself to the privilege and responsibility of fathering. The psalmist has given us a healthy perspective on the challenge before us:

Sons are a heritage from the Lord; children a reward from him. (Ps. 127:3)

True, there are moments when some of us wonder if our children are really a "reward" from the Lord! But when you think that Almighty God has entrusted to us the task of preparing young lives for responsible, worthwhile adulthood, the mission takes on eternal significance. Fathering is indeed a privilege given by the Lord—a matchless opportunity to pour our lives into those we love so dearly.

As we begin our journey together, I invite you to make the commitment with me that no matter how tough it may get, no matter how unresponsive your kids may be, no matter which way the road may bend in the future—we dedicate ourselves to the privilege and responsibility of conscientious, loving, involved, communicative fathering.

In the pages that follow, you will discover ten qualities that will help you become the kind of father you want to be, the kind of father your children need, the kind of father God calls you to be. You'll discover a whole new source of energy and insight into fatherhood, one that puts your role and responsibilities into perspective in a fresh, new way. And as you begin to experience the Father Connection, you'll begin to reap the benefits of the most rewarding job in the world.

A Special Note to Moms

I suspect that many moms will be reading this book—that's great! I know you'll gain valuable insights on effective fathering, but it need not stop there. I encourage you to take this initiative: urge your husband to read this book and be an encouragement to him as he does.

I want you to know that it's not my wish or purpose to downplay your important role in your children's lives by addressing this book to dads. I firmly believe in a team approach to parenting: Mom and Dad working together to raise their family. Unfortunately, I see too many dads defaulting on their responsibilities as parents. Too many men fail to take an active part in their children's lives, leaving the bulk of parenting to Mom.

So I've written this book to help us dads understand our God-given role and become true teammates with our wives in loving, instructing, guiding, cherishing, and affirming our children together.

If you're a single mom, you may be concerned about how your kids are affected by not having a father around (whether physically, emotionally, or both). If possible, share this book with your children's father. Keeping your kids' welfare in mind, help your "ex" to be the best possible dad he can be. It's in everyone's best interest, and your kids will love you for it.

If your children's father is no longer around or not a suitable dad, look for mature, godly men in your church who can provide a positive role model of Christian manhood for your kids. Perhaps another dad would be willing to include your kids in family outings or make special efforts to befriend and talk with your kids. You'll see from reading this book what a tremendous influence the father figure is in a child's life. In families where the father is absent, it's wise to try filling this void with a friend who can serve as a positive male role model to your kids.

And for all moms: you, more than anyone else, will determine how your children see their father. You have enormous power either to support Dad in his ministry to his children or to undermine him and make him look incompetent in their eyes. Encourage your husband in his attempts at fathering. He needs it. Be supportive in your words to him and your children. Lovingly confront his actions (or lack of action).

Mom, you're important! I'll be praying for you in your efforts to help Dad become all that God created him to be.

For Reflection, Discussion, and Action

1. Are you a full-time dad to your kids when you're home, or do you tend to remain preoccupied with thoughts of work or other things?

2. In what ways have you noticed yourself "defaulting" when it comes to the role of parenting? What important tasks are you leaving to their mother, to their teachers, to their youth workers that really should be your responsibility?

3. Were the survey results cited in this chapter surprising to you? Why or why not?

4. What would your children state is their primary source of information about truth and moral values?

5. Do your children enjoy the close personal relationship with you as their father that is pivotal to healthy child development? Why or why not?

*6. Dedicate yourself wholeheartedly to the privilege and responsibilities of Christian fathering. Study this book with pen in hand, underlining key thoughts and action points. Consider forming a small group of devoted dads to study and discuss these principles together.

*7. The most important thing I learned in this chapter was:

_____

_____

_____

_____

_____

*8. With my child, I need to start _____

_____

_____

_____

_____

*At the end of each chapter I have provided questions and action points to help you implement the principles from the chapter. If you have adequate reflection time, or if you are studying this book in a group with other men, I strongly recommend that you take the time to work through each question conscientiously. However, if time is a problem, work through only the questions marked by an asterisk (*).

CHAPTER 2
The Father Connection

If you're like most men, even those who had poor or harmful experiences with their own fathers, you have a general idea of the kind of father you want to be. You have a picture in your mind—perhaps sketchily drawn, but it's there nonetheless—of what the model father looks like:

- You want to be the kind of father whose children feel secure and confident, who feel loved and accepted.
- You want to be the kind of father whose children save sex for marriage and remain faithful to their husbands and wives in marriage.
- You want to be the kind of father whose sons and daughters develop a reputation as men and women of integrity—honest, ethical, and hardworking.
- You want to be the kind of father whose child might say, "My dad keeps his promises."
- You want to be the kind of father whose children stand up to unhealthy peer pressure, children who develop healthy friendships, children who earn the respect and admiration of their peers.

- You want to be the kind of father whose kids can say no to drug and alcohol abuse and risky behavior.
- You want to be the kind of father whose adult daughter sends a card just to say, "Dad, thanks for being there when I need you," the kind of father whose son asks you to be the best man at his wedding.
- You want to be the kind of father whose son can come and sit down beside him and say, "Dad, I'm really struggling with some things right now, and I need your advice."
- You want to be the kind of father whose children quickly admit their sins or mistakes, who are forgiving and patient with others, who enjoy a healthy sense of self-esteem and self-confidence.
- You want to be the kind of father who might overhear his daughter telling a friend, "I want to marry someone who's like my daddy, someone I can admire and respect."

That's the kind of father we all want to be. That's the kind of father I wanted to be as a young man. But I didn't know how. I knew my father wasn't *any* of those things when I was growing up, and I feared that I would become more like him than like the father I wanted to be. I knew that one of the things I needed was a model, a father I could pattern myself after, a father I could learn from and imitate. So I started looking around for men who looked like the kind of father I wanted to be. And I found them.

Looking for a Model

One of my earliest and most positive models of fatherhood was Dick Day, whom I mentioned earlier. I met Dick when we were both in seminary during the 1960s. Dick was a few years older than I was, and he was already married with four children. Like me, he was the son of an alcoholic father and the product of a dysfunctional home. He had come to Christ in his late twenties and had entered seminary in response to God's call to the ministry.

Dick and I met while registering for seminary classes, and the two of us hit it off immediately. We became fast friends. I soon became a virtual member of the Day family, often stopping by at odd hours, like 6:30 a.m. or after 11:00 p.m. to talk about something that I thought just couldn't wait. Dick was always patient, kind, and loving—traits that I had known little about while growing up.

I was impressed immediately by how Dick and Charlotte treated their children and each other. They had a rich and rewarding relationship with each of their children. I watched with amazement at the obvious joy they shared with each other, often smiling, laughing, and hugging. (In fact, you might say I learned to hug from hanging around with the Days.) I saw in Dick the kind of father I wanted to be someday. I saw a clear, concrete model of what I wanted to become.

Later, when Dick and I both joined the staff of Campus Crusade for Christ, we went in separate directions for a while. I began lecturing on college campuses around the U.S. and Canada and eventually met Dottie. As we began dating, I was intrigued by her frequent mention of her family and how much her mom, dad, brother, and sister obviously meant to her. During Christmas vacation a few months later, I met Dottie's family.

It's hard to say what drew me most in those early days of our relationship—getting to know Dottie or getting to know her dad. I began to understand why Dottie so admired her father. He was a conventional kind of guy, not flashy (a little straitlaced, as a matter of fact), but it was obvious why she loved and respected him so much. Right from the start, I learned from him what it means to be a loving husband and father. I saw a man who had his kids' love and respect, a man whose kids trusted him, a man whose kids were so well-raised that he could genuinely enjoy their company and bask in their friendship.

For years, these men filled my need for a model of the kind of father I wanted to be. They showed the qualities in a father that I had longed for all my life, the kind of qualities I desperately wanted to emulate someday in my own family. I benefited immeasurably from their example, but it wasn't until years later that I learned of a much better model, a much better way to become the father I wanted to be.

The Model Father

Norm Wakefield, the friend I mentioned in the first chapter, is one of the people who has helped me come to a meaningful and powerful realization about my role as a struggling father. Though Norm's childhood and teen experiences were different from mine, he shared some of my struggles in trying to form a healthy model of fatherhood. Norm explains it like this:

> It wasn't until I reached middle adulthood that I was able to establish a warm, friendly relationship with my father. My dad's career was filled with pressures and discouragements. He had difficulty enjoying his children, and we found it difficult to approach him.
>
> I remember placing my faith in Jesus Christ at age twelve—the first member of my family to become a Christian. But as I began to form a mental image of my heavenly Father's love for me, I couldn't help superimposing my relationship with my earthly father. Since my dad never seemed to be satisfied with me, I felt God must feel the same way. It was as if he were saying, "Norm, why don't you straighten up? Why do I have to put up with you? You'd better get your act together, young man, or I'm going to . . ."
>
> You can imagine the impact these ideas had on my self-image as a young teen, let alone my misperception of the love of God! It is very common for children to think God values them in the same way their own fathers regard them. If Dad is loving, warm, and nurturing, they tend to picture God as loving, warm, and nurturing. But if Dad is perceived as cold, distant and occupied with "more

important things," they are likely to feel that God is unapproachable and uninterested in them as individuals.

I had this mistaken image of God until my forties, when he brought some circumstances my way that literally transformed my relationship with him. I discovered what a loving, caring, vitally interested God he is! And interestingly enough, it was through these same circumstances that the walls finally came down, and my father and I were able to draw much closer together than we had ever been.

As part of my fresh discovery of the nature of God, I read through the Psalms with pen in hand, noting every mention of the Lord. As I studied these verses, I realized that almost every reference provided either a direct or indirect description of our heavenly Father. I soon had several notebook pages filled with these attributes, and from them emerged a profile of what most of us would consider an "ideal" father. My conclusion? The basic qualities of fatherhood that are seen in our Lord are the qualities he desires to form in today's Christian fathers.

I had discovered a theology of fatherhood—with God himself as the role model!

Yes, God is the model father! In my search for models of fatherhood, I had been fortunate to find two of the best. But Norm helped me see that I had neglected the greatest model of all—the original, the standard of effective fatherhood—God himself. The mental picture I had of the kind of father I wanted to be was actually a picture of my heavenly Father, who is the source of all good things (James 1:17).

He is "the Father, from whom all things came" (1 Cor. 8:6). He breathed the breath of life into the first man, and Adam became the first "son of God" (Luke 3:38). From that moment, each of us have been made in the likeness of our Father and Creator, who made us and formed us (Deut. 32:6). Literally from day one,

God has not only desired a Father-child relationship with each one of us, he has also modeled what a healthy fatherhood looks like.

He is a tender Father who invites us to address Him as "Abba," the Aramaic equivalent of "Daddy" or "Dada" (Rom. 8:15, Gal. 4:6). He is a listening Father who bids us to approach him boldly as "our Father in heaven" (Matt. 6:9). He is a loving Father who freely and forcefully demonstrated his Father-love at the baptism of his Son, Jesus, with a voice like thunder that said, "This is my Son, whom I love; with him I am well pleased" (Matt. 3:17). He is a giving Father who gives good gifts to his children (Matt. 7:11). He is the Father of all (Eph. 4:6), the very definition of fatherhood, the fount of everything that is good, moral, and worthy of imitation.

Therefore, if any man wants to become a good and effective father, the standard—the model—is God the Father. The characteristics I had longed for and missed in my own father were characteristics of God. The features I so admired in Dick Day and in Dottie's father were so attractive to me because they reflected the attributes of my heavenly Father. The qualities I yearned to display to my own children were the qualities that resembled my heavenly Father's nature.

This understanding, this realization, transformed and empowered me. I no longer had to feel crippled by my earthly father's example. I no longer had to search for models to imitate (though I could still benefit from their example and learn from their successes). I no longer had to struggle to form a clear picture of what a father should be, of the father I should be. All my needs as a father could be met in God, the Model Father!

The Father's Resource

As transforming as this realization was, however, I still had more to learn. And I have since been on a thrilling journey of discovery, determined to understand as much as I can about the Father qualities of God, knowing that such knowledge will not only deepen my awareness of him but also teach me what I need to know and be as a father to my children. As I strengthen my connection to God, I strengthen my connection to my children and enhance the effectiveness of my relationships and interaction with them.

The key to this two-sided Father Connection is the realization that God the Father is not only the incomparable *model* of effective fatherhood, he is the indispensable *resource* for becoming the father you long to be. The Father Connection is not mere imitation, not simple emulation; it is association. It isn't about knowing how; it's about knowing Who! The Father Connection isn't a new set of rules for fatherhood. There are plenty of books that simply add to your daily "to do" list, telling you what you *should* do or *would* do if you were a decent father. No, the Father Connection is about a relationship, one which—when applied to your role as a father—can transform you, your children, your family, and your future.

I found that the stronger my relationships with my four children were, the more they seemed able to counter peer pressure, make wise decisions, honor their father's wishes, and obey his rules. A strong, up-to-date relationship with Dad seems not only to make them more *willing* to live healthy, happy, godly lives, it seems to make them more *able* to do so. The confidence, security, and satisfaction that flow out of their relationship with their parents strengthens them against the traps and temptations they encounter when they're at school or with friends.

A similar thing happens on a much more profound level in my relationship with God the Father. When my relationship with him is strong and up-to-date, I am not only more *willing* to be the kind of father I want to be, I am literally *empowered* to do so through his Spirit, through his presence within me. In this crucial way, he is not only a role model for me as a father, but he is my resource as well.

To paraphrase Psalm 28:7, "He is my strength and my shield as a father; when my heart trusts in him, I am helped."

Making the Connection

A friend of mine tells the story of an experience he had as a teenage disk jockey at his high school radio station. The radio station operated throughout the summer, and it was Bob's job to come in around 7:30 in the morning and switch on the transmitter (a bulky hand-me-down from a commercial radio station which delivered the radio signal to the nearby tower, broadcasting to a whopping radius of about eight or ten miles). After a few minutes, the transmitter would be fully operational, and Bob would sign on at 8 a.m. for a four-hour show.

On this particular morning, Bob felt unusually sharp. His choice of music seemed inspired. His "segues"—the process of overlapping the end of one song with the beginning of the next—blended artfully. His banter between songs crackled with wit and wisdom. He was beginning to feel confident, even cocky . . . until he grabbed a clipboard to perform the hourly check of the meter readings on the transmitter.

The transmitter was dead.

Bob tapped the meters and jiggled the assorted wires that flowed to and from the transmitter. Then he glanced at the wall. The large electric plug dangled from the wall socket. The thing had somehow worked its way out and had been unplugged all morning! Bob's keen and clever performance had reached an audience of one—himself!—because the transmitter wasn't connected to the power source.

The chapters that follow highlight ten qualities of God the Father—every Christian's power source—that characterize his interaction with his children and provide a model for your role and tasks as a father. Each chapter will not only reveal a specific attribute of the Father but will help you apply and cultivate that quality with the help of God's Holy Spirit in your own life and family.

Join me in a commitment to model the character of our heavenly Father to our children. I believe it will be a commitment worth every bit of the time and energy that may be required, for you will not only be giving your children a beautiful picture of the Fatherhood of God. You will also be giving them a dad who is worthy of his kids' love and respect, a man whose kids trust him, a man who can genuinely enjoy the company of his children, take pride in them, and bask in their friendship.

For Reflection, Discussion, and Action

1. Take a few moments to contemplate the kind of father you want to be. Next, complete this statement as many times as necessary until you have a complete statement of your hopes and aims as a father. (Use a separate sheet of paper if necessary.)

I want to be the kind of father who _____
_____
_____

I want to be the kind of father who _____
_____
_____

I want to be the kind of father who _____
_____
_____

I want to be the kind of father who _____
_____
_____

I want to be the kind of father who _____
_____
_____

I want to be the kind of father who _____
_____
_____

I want to be the kind of father who _____
_____
_____

2. Who have been your most positive models of fatherhood? List them by name below and, beside each, list what their example has taught you.

_____

_____

_____

_____

_____

_____

_____

_____

_____

_____

_____

_____

_____

_____

_____

*3. How can you improve your relationship with your heavenly Father? Check any that apply:

❑ Beginning a regular habit of prayer and Bible reading
❑ Resuming a regular habit of prayer and Bible reading
❑ Continuing a regular habit of prayer and Bible reading
❑ Meeting regularly for worship and fellowship with others who love the Father
❑ Joining a prayer, Bible study, and/or accountability group

4. If you haven't already done so, select two or three other dads who will commit to forming an accountability group with you. Study this book and work through the questions together, and commit to praying for and encouraging each other toward excellence in Christian fathering.

CHAPTER 3
The Father's Unconditional Love and Acceptance

Several years ago, I had agreed to speak at a high school assembly in Phoenix, Arizona. Because of scheduling and space considerations, I had to speak to the entire student body at one time—a crowd too large to fit in the school auditorium. So the assembly was held outside, and I stood on a large rock to speak to the crowd of about a thousand students who sat on the grass in the schoolyard.

Just as I started to speak, a group of punk rockers, sporting fluorescent hair and wearing yards of chains, walked up to within twenty feet of where I stood. Some of the teachers and other students kept watchful eyes on the colorful group, perhaps expecting them to cause some kind of disturbance. But I continued my talk and finished speaking without interruption.

As soon as I stepped down off the rock, however, the apparent leader of the punk rockers ran up to me and planted himself less than a foot in front of me. A gasp arose from the crowd, and a thousand pairs of eyes were trained on me and that young man.

The majority of the crowd, however, couldn't see the tears that streamed down the punk rocker's face, nor could they hear him asking me to hug him. Soon a wave of murmurs rolled through the crowd as I threw my arms around that young man. He buried his head in my shoulder and cried.

The hug lasted about a minute—a long hug for a punk rocker! Finally, he let go of me and through his tears explained, "My father has never hugged me or said 'I love you.'"

That young man was crying out for a father's love. He wanted to feel the love and acceptance that only his father could give. His outlandish appearance and wild behavior were a cry for attention—something he wasn't getting from his father.

A Child's Most Basic Need

I have heard or witnessed similar stories hundreds, thousands of times. I have seen the pain and devastation that occurs in young men and women whose fathers are unwilling or incapable of communicating love and acceptance to their children.

I once spoke to a large number of teenagers at Fishnet, a large outdoor music festival and teaching conference held on a farm in Virginia. One morning while speaking about the importance and value of saving sex for marriage, I told the young people in the crowd of about 12,000 that they were special, that they should never forget they had immeasurable worth, and that someone who truly loved them would recognize their worth and honor it by waiting for marriage to have sex.

Later that morning, I noticed a young blonde girl about twelve years old following me. I stopped and asked, "Did you want to see me?"

She replied rather shyly, "Do you really think I'm special?"

"Yes!" I answered assuringly. "God made you special, and don't you ever forget it." I cautiously put my arms around her shoulders and gave her a tender, fatherly hug. She suddenly burst into tears.

"You don't know how long I've waited for that," she said. "My mom and dad divorced five years ago, and my dad has never hugged me or told me I'm special."

Five days later as I left for the airport, a note was slipped to me by a security man who said a little girl wanted me to have it. The tightly folded note had just six words written in red:

Thank you for loving me . . . Koreen.

That young woman was crying out for love and acceptance, the kind that only a father could give, the kind she had never received.

I can't tell you how many times my heart has been broken by the realization of how common Koreen's experience is. I have had countless young people say to me, "My father never shows any affection" or "My father only pays attention to me when I do something wrong."

I have heard fathers call their sons and daughters, "Stupid," "Dummy," or worse.

I have seen fathers scream derisively at their children on the baseball diamond or the basketball court.

I have eaten dinner with fathers who never spoke to their sons or included them in the conversation for an entire meal.

I have known fathers who spend very little time with their daughters, except to criticize what they're wearing or who they're dating.

I have observed fathers who talk candidly to others about their kids' faults and shortcomings, even when the kids are close enough to hear. And tragically, I have seen the emotional devastation that such fathers create in their own children by their actions or inaction.

Children, regardless of their age, have a deep-seated need to feel significant, accepted, and loved. God intends for this normal, healthy need to be met first in the home, by Dad and Mom. If both parents do not satisfy that hunger for love and acceptance, the young person will seek to fill that emotional void in someone or something else, leading to behaviors that can destroy or seriously cripple the child. A father who does not communicate love and acceptance to his child is not a *neutral* influence in his child's life; he is a *negative* one.

That's not the kind of father I wanted to be. I wanted to be the kind of father whose child feels accepted and loved, whose child grows into a secure, self-confident young man or woman, whose child is capable of loving and giving to others.

That's the kind of father my Father is.

First, Foremost, and Forever Love

I talk to many people, young and old, who don't realize that God loved them even before they became Christians. While we were in darkness, when we were still enemies of God, he loved us and died for us (see Eph. 5:8, Rom. 5:8). He loved us *first* (1 John 4:19). He did not wait for us to clean up our act. He did not wait for us to meet his expectations. He did not wait for us to make him proud. He simply loved us.

Not only that, but he *showed* his love for us. He is not the kind of father who has trouble hugging a child or saying "I love you." He is not the kind of father who has "more important things to do." He loves us *foremost* (Rom. 8:32). He spoke his love for us with the Word (John 1:14). He showed his love to us on a cross. He wrote his love for us in blood.

The Father not only loves us first and foremost, he also loves us *forever* (Jer. 31:3). The Father's love for us is complete, constant, and unconditional. We cannot earn it. We cannot escape it. We cannot erase it. He may be disappointed when we disobey him, or saddened when we stray from him, or sorrowful when we sin, but he never, never, never stops loving us. Our Father's unconditional love for us is such that . . .

> . . . neither death nor life, neither angels nor demons, neither the present nor the future, nor any powers, neither height nor depth, nor anything else in all creation, will be able to separate us from the love of God that is in Christ Jesus our Lord. (Rom. 8:38–39)

That's the kind of father I want to be, even of my grown children. I want my kids to know that I accept and love them. I want them to know that I loved them before they could return my love. I want them to know that I loved them when their primary interaction with me involved bottles, burps, and dirty diapers. I want them to know that my love for them is unconditional, not based on anything they do but on who they are.

I also want my children to know that my love for them is foremost. My job, my hobbies, my friends, my status in the church or community—none of these is more important to me than they are. My love for them is foremost.

Finally, I want to communicate to my children that I love them forever. I want them to know that I accept them and love them no matter what. They don't have to earn my love. They cannot escape my love. They cannot erase my love.

That's the kind of father I want to be. But, of course, that kind of fatherhood doesn't come naturally to many men, perhaps least of all to me. It's something I had to learn.

Creating a Climate of Love and Acceptance

Nothing is more important for a father to learn and give than unconditional love and acceptance. If your child does not feel this from you, he or she will not feel secure. An insecure child is seldom (if ever) willing to be vulnerable. The insecure child will not be transparent. He will not talk openly about what's happening at school. She will not share freely about how her date treated her. The more you communicate unconditional acceptance to your children, the more prone they will be to talk to you, to be open, to share their thoughts and concerns and struggles with you.

Of course, as I said, unconditional acceptance isn't easy. In fact, to be honest, it's not even possible. Only God can be totally accepting. We are limited as sinners in our ability to accept our children, but our weaknesses can be overcome by the power of the Holy Spirit, who gives us abilities we may not even know we have.

So how do we do it? How do we dads communicate unconditional love and acceptance to our children, the kind of love our Father demonstrates toward us?

It begins, of course, with heartfelt prayer and constant reliance on God. If we are connected to God through his Holy Spirit, we can then connect to our child's need by consciously and diligently implementing the following essentials of unconditional love and acceptance.

DEMONSTRATING AFFECTION

One of the most basic ways to meet a child's need for unconditional love is to demonstrate affection. There is immense power in a simple hug or kiss, a few fond words, or a loving look.

In his book *The Total Man*, Dan Benson reflects on the value of these moments in his childhood:

> I'll never forget the family hugs that often took place in our kitchen as I was growing up. Toddling through the doorway, I'd see Dad wrapping Mom in his arms (not an unusual sight in our home). That made me feel good inside. So good that I couldn't resist joining them. So I'd charge across the kitchen linoleum and wrap my arms around their legs. Mom and Dad were always happy to include me. If any other brothers were around, they would sometimes join in as the family hug got bigger and bigger. Mom and Dad made our house a loving home, more by example than by lecture. We were secure as children because Dad took the lead in making the home atmosphere one of love and joy.[1]

Demonstrative acts are not the same as unconditional love and acceptance, of course. Some parents who hug and kiss their children do not exhibit unconditional love and acceptance. However, hugs and kisses can help a father say to his kids, "I accept you and love you just as you are."

DELIGHTING IN EACH CHILD'S UNIQUENESS

God created each of us as unique individuals. Think of it: of the more than six billion people alive right now on planet earth, there is no one just like you. And there is no one just like your son or daughter.

Dottie's father, whom I mentioned in chapter 2, had simple ways to recognize each child as an individual. He would say to Dottie, "You're my favorite big girl." Then he would say to her younger sister, "You're my favorite little girl." To her brother he would say, "You're my favorite boy." It may seem simple, even silly, but it works, and it is one way he made his children feel special.

It's a tragedy to hear a father tell a child, "Why can't you be more like your brother?" or "Your sister never had this kind of trouble in math!" How much better to delight in each child's uniqueness by recognizing him or her as an individual with singular traits, talents, and gifts. If you start studying your own children, you'll find many ways each one is unique: a contagious laugh, a skill for making friends, a compassionate spirit, a pretty singing voice, a radiant smile, a love for animals. Be sure to communicate the glories and wonder of that uniqueness to your child in positive ways.

AFFIRMING YOUR CHILD'S PERSONAL WORTH

Your child needs a sense of personal worth. A person must gain the belief and feeling that he is a person of value.

Fathers can communicate a child's personal worth in many ways. One of the most important ways is to spend time with the child. Time communicates importance. In fact, I've often said that kids spell love differently than their parents; they spell it "T-I-M-E." This was a particular challenge for me because I was away from home about half the time. I worked hard to compensate, however, taking my children on the road with me whenever possible, calling home every day, and taking the kids out to breakfast when I returned from a trip.

One Sunday, I was invited to speak to the San Diego Chargers in their pre-game chapel. I took my son Sean, and after chapel we found our seats in the stadium. The team had given us seats down front, near the fifty-yard line! Fifty thousand spectators filled the stadium and the roar was deafening.

I put my arm around my son and said, "Look at all these people, buddy." Sean turned 360 degrees in his seat to see everyone, especially those way up high. To those ten-year-old eyes it looked like the whole world was there.

"Wow, Dad," Sean exclaimed, "that's a lot of people!"

"Yes, it is. But you know what? You mean more to me than all these people put together. And what you think of me as your dad means more to me than the opinion of all fifty thousand people!"

Sean's eyes grew big. Again he surveyed the entire stadium. Then, with his childish excitement, he exclaimed: "Really, Dad? More than all them?" He jumped on my lap, feeling very secure and significant.

At that moment, Sean knew he counted with me.

FOSTERING A SENSE OF BELONGING

If our children don't feel they belong at home, they will look elsewhere for a place to belong. Some, like the punk rocker I met in Phoenix, identify with an outlandish peer group. Others join street gangs for the sense of belonging they offer. Still others try to fill their need for acceptance with sexual encounters.

Sue, a high school junior, explained her sexual activity this way: "I felt so alone. Mom and Dad were always too busy to have time for me. When Ted befriended me, I was ecstatic. He listened to me. He would hold me and console me. He really seemed to care about me."

My friend Dick Day and his wife, Charlotte, whom I mentioned in the previous chapter, adopted a Korean orphan whom they named Timothy. After Timmy arrived in America and became part of the Day household, he spent many months adjusting to his new family and American culture. One day, when Timmy was still struggling somewhat with the adjustments, Dick asked him, "Timmy, would you ever like to go back to Korea?"

"Oh, no," Timmy answered.

"Why not?" Dick asked.

"Because here," Timmy said, "I am somebody special."

You, too, can give your children that sense of belonging, the feeling that they are an important part of your family. Having that emotional haven will give them strength to withstand feelings of insecurity, negative peer pressure, and sexual temptation. Your love and acceptance says, "You belong—you are valued," and gives them a basis on which to value and esteem themselves.

ACKNOWLEDGING VALUE MORE THAN PERFORMANCE

When my son Sean was twelve, he played on a little league baseball team. A week before the season started, I got an idea about how to show him and his teammates acceptance. I bought twelve coupons good for ice cream sundaes at a local restaurant, and took them to his coach.

"Coach," I said, "these are for the kids."

"Thanks," the coach said with a big smile. "This is great. I wish more dads took an interest like this. I'll take them for sundaes after their first win."

"No, coach," I said quickly. "I want you to take them for sundaes after their first loss."

He looked at me strangely. I could see that what I had said didn't compute with his concept of winning, losing, and rewards for good play. Then I explained.

"Coach, I don't know about you," I said, "but as I raise my kids, I don't want to acknowledge their success as much as their effort. And I don't want to acknowledge their effort as much as their being created in the image of God. I believe my son is created in the image of God and that he has infinite value, dignity, and worth, which all have nothing to do with playing baseball. If he never played an inning of baseball in his life, I would love and accept him just as much."

Sean's coach studied me for a long moment. Finally, all he could muster was, "Well, that's novel."

The coach was true to his word. After the team's first loss, he gave each player a coupon and they went out for ice cream sundaes as a team.

Sean must have thanked me at least five times for the sundaes. In addition, over the next two weeks, three of the kids on his team thanked me for the special treat. I especially recall one boy named Jessie, who said, "Thanks a lot for the ice cream sundaes, Mr. McDowell. Wow! It doesn't matter to you if we win or not—you love us anyway."

That, of course, was the point. I wanted to communicate to Sean and his teammates that I loved, accepted, and valued them regardless of how well they performed, based upon the fact that they are each created in the image of God and, consequently, possess infinite value and dignity.

CULTIVATING A SENSE OF COMPETENCE

Children need a growing sense of competence in order to feel loved and accepted in their family and in society. All children have a natural desire to do well. As parents, we can encourage our children in their attempts and congratulate them on their accomplishments. Unfortunately, there are several reasons why a child may not achieve his sense of competence easily.

Adults tend to measure a child's ability by adult standards. We can't expect a child to function at our adult level of competence. I couldn't expect my daughters to wash the car as well as I could. When my son was younger, I couldn't expect him to make his bed as neatly as I did. I had to give consideration to their limited knowledge and understanding.

Neither can we expect our children to be competent without training. How many skills are involved in making a bed, washing a car, and mowing the lawn? Yet many parents assign tasks without giving adequate guidance: "You're old enough to clean your own room now. Do it! And do it right!"

When you do give your children guidance on a task, you also need to give them the freedom to fail. Should they fail, you need to encourage them to complete the task, perhaps with your help. Praise what has been accomplished and motivate your child to finish the task left undone: "The outside of the car looks great! You did a nice job. But the inside needs some sprucing up. How about if I help you vacuum the inside?"

There are influences outside your family which affect your child's sense of competence as well. We live in a competitive society. We constantly find ourselves pitted against others and their abilities on the job, at school, on the athletic field. Unfortunately, there is always someone who does things just a little better than we do. Many of us are far down the ladder of competence in some areas of our lives, so when we are consistently measured against superior performers, our self-confidence is easily eroded.

Nourishing a sense of competence in our children is a long-term effort that requires much thought and planning. It also requires that we become positive models ourselves, slow to find fault and quick to affirm new levels of growth. We need to help them embrace a true assessment of their strengths and accept their limitations without self-condemnation.

A father has a singular opportunity to create a positive environment in the home; one that draws out his children's strengths, nurtures and reinforces them, and instills within his children a keen sense of who they are and why they possess infinite value, worth, and dignity. Such children will be less inclined to become sexually active before marriage. They will be far less likely to turn to unhealthy relationships in a search for love and acceptance. They will be less likely to rebel. They will be less likely to succumb to peer pressure. By the same token, such kids will be more inclined to strong sexual standards. They will be more likely to develop healthy relationships. They will be more apt to succeed in school and, later, in business.

Such things are a father's dream, of course. But they do not happen by accident. They do not even happen as a result of human effort. They can only happen when we are connected—through prayerful reliance on the Holy Spirit—to the Father who loves and accepts us, and who enables us by careful and diligent effort to be the kind of fathers we want to be, the kind of father our Father is to us.

For Reflection, Discussion, and Action

1. After I related the story about the twelve-year-old girl named Koreen, I mentioned several negative or destructive things I have seen, heard, or known fathers to say or do. Review the list on page 27. Do you identify with any of these behaviors or tendencies? If so, take some time to consider how these behaviors might affect your child's awareness of your love and acceptance.

2. Why are your children special in God's sight? Think of each child by name, and list at least five specific reasons why each is special to God and to you. Then devise ways you can communicate those things to each child.

_____

_____

_____

_____

_____

_____

*3. Think of each of your children by name. Does that child know that you love and accept him or her? How do you know?

*4. Think of two things you can do for each of your children this week that will communicate how you accept and love him or her, based not on what he or she *does* but on who he or she *is*. When and how will you implement these ideas?

_____

_____

_____

_____

_____

_____

CHAPTER 4
The Father's Purity

Some time ago, I received a letter from a Christian father who had heard me speak. He said that he and his wife had always done their best to be good parents. They were members of a good church and had always been proud of their children. But he told me they had just discovered something about their oldest daughter, something that brought their world crashing down around them.

This father described his teenage daughter as a pretty girl, but said that she'd never been real popular with boys. Until recently. She had started dating one of the football players, and very early in the relationship (this father had just learned) she'd had sex with the boy. She then went from that football player to another. Before long, her father told me, she had slept with the whole football team.

"Josh," this tortured father wrote, "they were passing my little girl around as some sort of 'team girl'!"

It's a father's nightmare. No father wants to be in that man's shoes. No father wants his child to be sexually vulnerable or become sexually active before marriage. No father wants his child to be sexually unfaithful *during* marriage.

But what can we do to reduce the chances of such a nightmare happening in our lives? How can we increase the likelihood that our sons and daughters will make wise choices in sexual matters? Where do we turn? How can we help?

The Father Factors

Fathers have the first and potentially greatest opportunity to shape a child's sexual convictions and behavior. According to the research, a father's influence is felt at three points:

1. *A father's presence.* Jerry Adler reported that more than half of all American children today are expected to spend part of their childhood with just their mothers. "A Census Bureau study found that 16.3 million American children were living with just a mother . . . and 40 percent of those hadn't seen their father in at least a year."[1] This is a critical statistic, because the absence or presence of a father in the home is a determining factor in a child's sexual attitudes and actions. As was mentioned in the first chapter, Johns Hopkins University researchers have reported that "young, white teenage girls living in fatherless homes . . . were 60 percent more likely to have premarital intercourse than those living in two-parent homes."[2] But the effects of a father's absence from the home are felt by the boys, as well. Researcher Robert Billingham of Indiana University suggests that boys who grow up without a live-in dad "may model more from cultural stereotypes of how a man is supposed to behave, from TV and movies' short-term seductions."[3]

2. *A father's attention.* In his book *Father: The Figure and the Force*, Christopher Andersen cites a study of 7,000 women working in topless bars and strip clubs. While economic considerations may certainly have influenced their choice of employment, Andersen wrote, "Most of these women conceded that they were probably looking for the male attention they had never gotten during their childhood."[4] Andersen goes on to suggest a direct correlation between the absence of paternal attention and these women's sexual behavior.

3. *A father's closeness.* Two specific studies commissioned by Josh McDowell Ministries both strongly indicated that sexual activity and promiscuity were much less likely among teenagers (both male and female) who reported close relationships with their fathers. These and many other studies suggest that a healthy relationship with Dad is a critical factor in whether or not young men and women engage in premarital sexual activity.

The Third Greatest Influence

If any one of these three father factors are absent or lacking, Dad will become a distant third behind the following two elements that compete to influence a young person's sexual standards. They are:

PEER PRESSURE

The peer group, of course, has a formidable influence on youth. Our youth culture communicates its own message concerning personal worth, sexuality, identity, and acceptance. In his book *The Kid-Friendly Dad*, author Frank Martin recounts a story he heard from a renowned family counselor:

> A sixteen-year-old girl was sent to him for counseling, and while there described her first sexual encounter at the age of thirteen. "I was so tired of hearing about sex from my friends and wanted to know what it was like for myself," she began. "So at a party I went up to the cutest guy I could find and asked him if he wanted to do it." The two of them went into a bedroom, and in a matter of moments this young, innocent girl had lost her virginity. "It wasn't what I expected," she told the counselor. "But at least I knew what it was like and was able to talk about it with my friends."[5]

The power of peer pressure is a major determinant in a teen's sexual activity, particularly if that young person is missing one or more of the three father factors mentioned above. A study of a thousand teens showed that 76 percent would go far enough sexually to feel experienced and not feel left out.[6] In many of our kids' communities, schools, and peer groups, the pressure to join the "sex derby" can be formidable.

MEDIA MESSAGES

The nationwide study of teens that spawned our ministry's "Why Wait?" campaign, promoting purity and sexual abstinence before marriage, showed that peers are the number-one influence on our kids' sexual attitudes and behavior. But what influences the peers? The majority of their peers learned about sex and sexuality not from parents, not from church, not from school, but from the steady stream of TV, movies, rock music, and periodicals that are more shallow and explicit today than ever before.

Television. The media is perhaps the greatest determinant in the evangelical teenager's sexuality. What gives the media such power over young people? Consider these facts: The average preschooler spends more time watching television than a university student spends in the classroom earning a bachelor's degree. One study revealed that preschool children watch twenty hours of TV per week; grade school children watch twenty-two hours. "Sleeping is the only activity that commands more of their time. By the age of eighteen, they will have spent more time in front of the TV set than anywhere else, including school."[7] Another study estimates that by graduation, the average high school student has spent 22,000 hours watching TV, which is twice the amount of time spent in the classroom during twelve years of school.

Music. From grades seven to twelve, kids listen to an average of 10,500 hours of rock music. The total amount of time spent in school over a period of twelve years is just 500 hours more than the time spent listening to rock music.[8] "Teenagers are inordinately influenced by the media. They have less interaction with real adults than ever before, so their friends and the role models presented in the media have an even greater impact."[9]

Movies and videos. Most of our young people have developed their concept of sexuality based upon this media fiction without realizing the price tag that comes with free love and casual sex. If they are unable to revise their convictions, they eventually will pay a high price. A young lady tells of that price:

> What the movies and the soap operas don't tell us about is the devastation and the broken hearts that occur due to affairs and premarital sex. I don't make light of the consequences of wrong sexual involvement. Without a doubt, the hardest and most painful thing I've gone through . . . more than major surgery, tests for cancer, a broken family, and numerous job rejections . . . is getting over a sexual relationship with a married man.[10]

Those words break my heart. They scare me. I hope they scare you, too—enough to make you want to help your kids counter the effects of peer pressure and media messages, to make you more determined than ever to become and remain, not the third greatest influence, but the greatest influence in the formation of your children's views on sex and sexuality.

I challenge you to be the kind of father whose children know God's view about sex, whose children possess healthy, wholesome attitudes about sexuality. Be the kind of father who talks to his children about sex and purity, and who can brace them for the pressures and temptations they are sure to face as teenagers and young adults. Be the kind of father whose children are empowered to save sex for marriage and who will remain faithful to their husbands and wives for life. Be the kind of father our Father is.

The Model of Purity

The precepts of God throughout his Word command purity for his people. God has spoken through the law, and he has made his standard clear: sexual impurity (that is, any sexual activity outside of marriage) is wrong:

Abstain . . . from sexual immorality. (Acts 15:29)

Flee from sexual immorality. (1 Cor. 6:18)

We should not commit sexual immorality. (1 Cor. 10:8)

Among you there must not be even a hint of sexual immorality . . . because these are improper for God's holy people. (Eph. 5:3)

Put to death, therefore, whatever belongs to your earthly nature: sexual immorality [and] impurity. (Col. 3:5)

It is God's will that you . . . should avoid sexual immorality. (1 Thess. 4:3)

It's hard to miss God's concern for purity. But what *is* often missed is the fact that such concern not only reveals what God commands, it also reveals what he values. God values purity. He has continually striven to communicate this value to his people: he demanded the use of pure gold in the construction of the tabernacle; he prescribed pure incense for use in worship; he required pure animals for sacrifice; he commanded pure hearts (Matt. 5:8), pure religion (James 1:27), and pure relationships (1 Tim. 5:2).

But even more than that, this precept reveals something about God himself: the Model Father is pure. "Everyone who has this hope in him purifies himself, just as he is pure" (1 John 3:3). Thomas Trevethan describes the purity of God in memorable terms:

The true God is distinct, set apart, from all that is evil. His moral perfection is absolute. His character as expressed in his will forms the absolute standard of moral excellence. God is holy, the absolute point of reference for all that exists and is good. Across the board he is to be contrasted with his creatures. At heart he is a glowing-white center of absolute purity.[11]

Because God is pure, sexual impurity is an offense against him. King David, who sinned with Bathsheba, later repented, confessing to God, "Against you, you only, have I sinned and done what is evil in your sight" (Ps. 51:4). Was David ignoring the fact that his sin had affected other people, resulting in the death of Bathsheba's husband, Uriah, and of the baby Bathsheba bore David? No, he was acknowledging the fundamental fact that when he sinned with Bathsheba, he sinned against the Lawgiver. His act was wrong because it offended God's purity.

In other words, the Model Father communicates—in contrast to modern culture, peer pressure, and media messages—that purity is good. The Model Father commands purity because purity is something he values. And purity is something he values because he himself is pure.

That's the kind of father we should want to be. Help your kids to know that purity is good, not something to be ashamed of or embarrassed about. Help them reject the fascination with immorality and deviancy that their culture and peers and the media so often display. And help them know that you value purity, like the Father you serve and seek to emulate. Help them see a godly standard of sexual purity in you.

This is easier said than done, of course. But then, nobody can do it in the first place. It requires prayerful reliance on the Holy Spirit, who then can work in and through your efforts as you employ some sound strategies, such as these:

SHOWING ATTENTION AND AFFECTION

I once held a week-long conference at one of the largest and wealthiest evangelical churches in the U.S. While there, I had counseling appointments with forty-two junior and senior high school students. Their number one question was, "Josh, what can I do about my dad?" When I asked what they meant, they made statements like, "He never has time for me," "He never takes me anywhere," "He never talks to me," and "He never does anything with me." I asked all forty-two kids, "Can you talk with your father?" Only one said yes.

These young people were starved for attention and affection from their fathers. This kind of "love famine" can affect both parents and children, creating a vicious self-perpetuating cycle in which parents who are starved for love raise children who are even hungrier for love. And the results can be devastating.

Your child needs your attention. When my kids were still in our home, I often used to pick them up at school and take them out for lunch. A thirty-minute walk in the neighborhood or a quick trip to Dairy Queen for an ice cream cone can provide opportunities to pay attention to your kids and communicate that they're important to you. My friend Norm Wakefield talks about one of his experiences when his children were young:

Once, when my family was eating lunch on a Sunday afternoon after church, I said to the kids, "I'm going to give each of you a gift today." Their eyes lit up with eager, inquisitive expressions. "I'm going to give each of you thirty minutes. I'll do whatever you want to do during that time." Their response was a squeal of delight as energetic as if I had presented an attractively wrapped gift.

I asked Amy what she would like to do. "I want to go for a walk with you, Daddy." So we walked through our neighborhood, hand in hand, and stopped for an ice cream cone.

When we returned home, Joel said that he wanted to wrestle on the front lawn. So we wrestled for thirty minutes.

Then I asked Jill, who was preparing to enter kindergarten, what she wanted to do. "I'd like to sit on your lap on the back porch lounge chair and have you read to me." So we read.

That afternoon I learned how significant the gift of time is to our children. When it is given eagerly and generously, it pays rich dividends.

Your children—regardless of their age—need your affection. I really believe that hugs between fathers and teen sons and daughters could do more to encourage the development of sexual purity in teens than any other single factor. You can't hug your kids enough, you really can't. It doesn't matter how old or how big they are; no one ever outgrows the need for affection. There is awesome power in a simple thing like a hug, a wink, and a whispered or pantomimed, "I love you!"

BEING OPEN ABOUT SEXUAL SUBJECTS

The communication process between you and your son or daughter is essential if your children are to profit from you in their pilgrimage toward healthy sexual attitudes and behavior.

You and your wife have the first and best chance to guide your child toward personal wholeness. If open and positive communication channels are maintained, the richness of your own sexual security will color the relationship. Your son will learn from you what it means to be a man and how he should treat a woman. He will feel comfortable about himself because he has had one of the best guides available. Your daughter will gain self-respect and cherish her femininity as she hears you express your delight in her. As she grows older, she will have a sound basis by which to measure other men with whom she relates. She will be less vulnerable to the exploits of men because the authority of your own life and love will provide a defense. She will learn how to relate to those of the opposite sex.

Your ability to express and talk about the sexual aspect of life is a vital element in your relationship with your children. We can learn a lesson about discussing personal purity and sexual morality with our children from the Bible. In Proverbs 3–7, children are instructed to listen to the wisdom of their parents about sexual matters. The parents are never admonished or commanded to talk to their children about sex. It is assumed that the parents *will* talk to their children. Have you followed through on communicating with your children about this very important part of their lives?

The importance of communication in the area of sexuality raises one issue all dads need to face. If we are uncertain or uncomfortable with our own sexuality, we will communicate this to our children. If a man was raised in an environment that belittled women, he may communicate attitudes and feelings to his daughters that will leave them vulnerable to men. If you were taught that men are to be strong, silent, tough, and insensitive, your sons may pick up these same tendencies by observing you.

But remember, we don't have to be trapped by destructive, negative communication patterns. Through the empowering of God's Spirit, we really *can* form new, liberating feelings, attitudes, and actions that communicate to our children a joyful, loving way of life.

MODELING GODLY STANDARDS OF PURITY

Your children will more easily develop godly standards of purity if they see their father modeling God's standards of purity. A father who consistently treats his wife with kindness, affirms her womanhood, and cherishes her as a life partner lays a powerful foundation of emotional stability in his children. A father who keeps himself separate from the world's values of sex—in how he acts, what he views, and what he listens to—models God's purity to his children.

One of the most effective ways to build godly standards of purity in your children is to let them see what a healthy image of sex looks like. Many parents are so reserved or embarrassed about sex that they give their children the idea that sex—even sex within the commitment of marriage—is dirty (or, at least, "something we don't talk about"). But letting your kids know that sex is part of the pure, beautiful relationship you enjoy with your wife encourages healthy attitudes toward sex the way God designed it. In our book *How to Be a Hero to Your Kids*, Dick Day and I shared the following story:

> Dick recalls the time Charlotte had been back in the Midwest speaking to a women's conference at Wheaton College. She had been gone about a week and was coming into San Diego on a six o'clock flight. As he prepared to drive from Julian down to San Diego—about sixty miles—he said to Timmy and Jonathan, then in their early teens, "Guys, would it be okay if you spend the night here by yourselves? Your brother is just down the street, and you can call him if you have a problem. I'd like to pick up Mom and spend the night in San Diego at a hotel."
>
> Timmy looked at his dad, then got a big grin on his face. He gave Dick a gentle nudge in the ribs and with eyes sparkling he said, "Go for it, Dad! Go for it!"[12]

Dick's sons saw in their parents' relationship an image of sex that reinforced the beauty and purity of sex the way God designed it—within marriage.

TEACHING GODLY STANDARDS OF PURITY

When my daughter Kelly turned fifteen, I did something I had looked forward to for years. I took Kelly on a series of dates. I asked her out, then dressed up and left the house so I could then swing by to pick her up. I opened and closed the car door for her, took her to a nice restaurant, held her chair for her, and initiated dinner conversation about her interests. After dinner, we went to a fun activity of her choice.

At the end of each date, I took a few moments to explain to Kelly that the way I treated her that night is the way a boy should treat her if he genuinely respects and cares for her. Since that time, I have taken my two other daughters out on dates. My wife, Dottie, was also our son Sean's first date. I coached him on what to do, how to treat her, and how to honor her throughout the evening.

Those date nights are just one technique I've used to teach godly standards of purity to my children. I have also used opportunities presented by TV, movies, current events, and the weddings of family and friends as occasions to discuss God's standards for sexual purity with my kids. I've even enlisted *graffiti* in my teaching efforts, pointing to a certain four-letter-word that was spray-painted on a wall, explaining to my kids why *that word*—which degrades something God intended to be beautiful—is so offensive, going on from there to teach them about the purity and sanctity of sex in the context of a marriage relationship.

SHARING THE BENEFITS OF PURITY

One of the most powerful ways to encourage the development of personal standards of purity in your kids—standards that reflect the purity of God himself—is to share with them the *benefits* of purity (as well as the consequences of immorality) at every opportunity.

Every chance I got, I tried to let my children know that godly standards of purity are the surest path to pleasure and fulfillment, and that immorality is the surest path to feelings of guilt, disappointment, and emptiness. I reminded them that God's standard of purity protects them from unplanned pregnancies and sexually transmitted diseases, while also providing peace of mind. I tried to impress on them that sexual purity protects them from sexual insecurity and provides an atmosphere of trust between a husband and wife. I shared with my kids how purity before and during marriage makes for true intimacy between a husband and wife, protecting them from the consequences that immorality breeds: suspicion, disappointment, sorrow, stress, emptiness, and many other destructive emotions.

My daughter Katie once said to me, very soberly, "Daddy, thanks for loving me."

"What do you mean?" I asked.

"You've always told me the truth," she said, without hesitation. "You've talked to me about sex and consequences, and I know so many kids who are making wrong choices. They just don't realize the consequences." She went on to say she wished all her friends and classmates had a dad who talked openly to them about the benefits of purity and the consequences of impurity.

As fathers, you and I have a momentous and holy job to do: to foster within our children a realization, respect, and reflection of God's standard of purity. It is a job that begins with the work of the Holy Spirit in our own lives—his enabling power being added to our efforts—to show attention and affection to our children, to be open with them about sexual subjects, to model godly standards of purity ourselves, to consciously teach godly standards of purity, and to share the benefits of purity at every opportunity.

As you do that with God's help, your children will be empowered to resist the pressure—from peers, from society, from their own hormones—to become sexually active before marriage.

They will be better equipped to develop and maintain a healthy, godly view of sex.

They will more likely be spared the heartache and tragedy that so often follows unwise decisions in the area of sexuality.

They will be better prepared later in life to remain faithful to their husbands and wives in marriage.

Not only that, you will also connect with your children in a way that will make you the kind of father you want to be—the kind of father your *Father* wants you to be.

For Reflection, Discussion, and Action

1. What kind of influence do you think peers are having on your children's sexual attitudes? What about the media? You? Be specific.

_____

_____

_____

_____

2. Review the five strategies for fostering godly standards of purity that are mentioned in this chapter. Place an x on each of the lines below, indicating how you rate your current success in those five areas:

I give attention and show affection to my children.

_____

always   sometimes   **never**

I exhibit openness about sexual subjects.

_____

always   sometimes   **never**

I model godly standards of purity.

_____

always   sometimes   **never**

I teach godly standards of purity.

_____

always   sometimes   **never**

I share the benefits of purity and the consequences of impurity.

_____

always   sometimes   **never**

3. Identify two of the areas from the previous list in which you would like to see improvement, and consider what you can do to improve. Are there any ideas you can garner from the suggestions and illustrations in this chapter that might help? If so, underline those ideas and make plans to implement them as soon as possible.

*4. Have at least two "Dates with Dad" with each of your children during the next six weeks. Plan something they want to do, then devote your full attention to them during that time. Make it fun—for both of you!

What will you do on the first date?_____
_____
_____

When is the date planned? _____
_____
_____

What will you do on the second date? _____
_____
_____

When is *that* date planned?_____
_____
_____

CHAPTER 5
The Father's Truth

When my daughter Kelly was in fourth grade, several students in her class swiped an object off the teacher's desk while the teacher was out of the room. The children only wanted to play with the object, but it soon broke, and they returned it to its previous place on the teacher's desk.

When the teacher returned to the classroom and discovered the damage, she asked one of Kelly's classmates what had happened. The girl yielded to the pressure of the group and lied. Then the teacher turned to Kelly, who answered the teacher's questions directly and honestly, despite the unspoken pressure from her classmates to protect them as the other girl had done.

The next day, I took Kelly out for breakfast at our favorite restaurant, and told her I was proud of her because she'd done the right thing in spite of any pressure she might have felt or any harassment she might have gotten from her classmates.

I have been pleased and proud many times as a result of my children's honesty and integrity, particularly because I realize how rare these character traits are. Cheating is pervasive among today's high school students. In a survey of high school juniors and seniors with an A or B average, nearly 80 percent admitted to some dishonesty, such as copying another student's homework or cheating on a test.[1] A national survey of teens and "twenty-somethings" indicates that nearly half (44 %) believe that "lying is sometimes necessary."[2] And shoplifting (as well as other forms of stealing) among teens is fashionable in some schools and communities.

Those types of behaviors and attitudes are not confined just to "problem kids" either. They're shockingly common among churchgoing kids, Christian kids, and kids who come from Christian families.

The study that spawned the *Right from Wrong* campaign revealed disturbingly high levels of deceit and dishonesty among Christian youth. Our survey of 3,795 teens in evangelical Christian churches indicated that two of every three (66%) said they had lied to a "parent, teacher, or other older person" within the previous three months. Slightly fewer—six in ten (59%)—said they had lied to a friend or peer within the last three months. More than one-third (36%) admitted they had cheated on an exam or other evaluation within that same three month period, and nearly one-sixth (15%) said they had recently stolen money or other possessions.

The research indicates that our young people see deceit as an easy way to get ahead. They view dishonesty as a means of impressing their peers and gaining approval from their parents. They're not even convinced it's wrong, and they seldom see the negative consequences of deceit nor the positive results of honesty.

But you want your children to know better, don't you? You want your sons and daughters to become men and women of integrity. You don't want them to cheat and lie, to you or to anyone else. You don't want them to take things that don't belong to them, whether it's an illegal music download or time from an employer. You want them to speak the truth, to live quiet and honest lives, to mind their own business, and to work in such a way that their daily lives will win the respect of others (1 Thess. 4:11–12).

And you want to be the kind of father who teaches, trains, and models that kind of life, whose children remember his honesty and sincerity and who respect him for his integrity.

You want to be the kind of father your Father is.

The Father Image

Thousands of years ago, God appeared to Moses on a remote mountain in the Sinai peninsula and issued these commands:

You shall not steal. You shall not give false testimony against your neighbor. (Exod. 20:15–16)

In the course of his revelation to Moses, God reiterated, amplified, and applied those precepts:

Do not steal. Do not lie. Do not deceive one another. Do not swear falsely. . . . Do not defraud your neighbor or rob him. (Lev. 19:11–13)

God strove to make it abundantly clear to his people—by precept—that lying, cheating, and stealing were wrong. But those commands also reveal a principle that God values: the principle of honesty, the quality of being truthful, transparent, and trustworthy. God values honesty; "The LORD detests lying lips," Solomon wrote, "but he delights in men [and women] who are truthful" (Prov. 12:22).

The principle of honesty does not possess intrinsic value; it is a virtue simply because it springs from the nature and character of God. Do you remember the day I talked about at the beginning of this chapter, when I took my daughter out to breakfast to congratulate her for being honest in a difficult situation? I tried to accomplish more that morning than just praising her moral behavior.

"Honey," I asked her, after telling her how proud I was of her, "why is lying wrong?"

"Because the Bible says it's wrong," she stated confidently.

"But," I pressed her, "why does the Bible say it's wrong?"

"Because God commanded it," she answered.

"But why did God command it?" I asked.

She looked at me as though I'd asked the question in a foreign language. Finally, she answered, "I don't know."

I took her hands in mine and locked eyes with her. I wanted to be sure she understood and remembered what I was about to tell her. "Because God is truth, Kelly. Truth comes from his nature, and whatever is contrary to God's nature is sin."

Honesty is right (and dishonesty wrong) for only one reason: because God is true. Truth is not something God does, nor is it something he possesses; it is a part of who he is. In the wilderness of Horeb, Moses sang, "He is the Rock, his work is perfect . . . a God of truth and without iniquity, just and right is he" (Deut. 32:4, KJV).

He is the God "who does not lie" (Titus 1:2). When God speaks a promise, you may count on it because "it is impossible for God to lie" (Heb. 6:18). Though honesty may go begging on earth, as the early Roman poet Juvenal said, there is an eternal, universal standard of truth that will not waver or change: "Let God be found true," the Bible says, "though every man be found a liar" (Rom. 3:4, NASB).

Because God is true, lying is an offense against his nature. Because God is true, cheating is an affront to him. Because God is true, stealing is an insult to him. God is true, and there is nothing false in him. It is his nature that defines honesty as moral, dishonesty as fraud, and theft as evil.

I want my children to understand that God is true—that whatever is like God is good, and whatever is unlike him is evil. I want to reflect the image of the true God in my fathering, and for my kids to reflect his image in their honesty and integrity. I want them to understand that the reason why honesty is the best policy is because it pleases God, reflects his nature, and shows his image to others.

Once again, the key to achieving all of this is the Father Connection we've been talking about. It requires us to be connected to the Father through prayer, daily devotion, and obedience to Him. Then we can begin to make the Father Connection with our own children, as we show them the Father's image in concrete ways, such as:

MODELING A LIFE OF INTEGRITY

God gave Israel a model for teaching truth to our children when he said:

> Hear, O Israel! The LORD is our God, the LORD is one! You shall love the LORD your God with all your heart and with all your soul and with all your might. These words, which I am commanding you today, shall be on your heart. You shall teach them diligently to your sons [and daughters] and shall talk of them when you sit in your house and when you walk by the way and when you lie down and when you rise up. (Deut. 6:4–8, NASB, with my one addition)

God makes it clear that if we want to pass on biblical values like honesty to our children, we must model these values in our own lives. His words must be on our hearts before we can impress them upon the hearts and minds of our children. In his book *Pulling Weeds, Planting Seeds*, Dennis Rainey says of his father:

> As an impressionable young boy, my radar caught more of Dad's life than he ever knew. During my perilous teenage years, he was the model and hero I needed—and he still is. He taught me the importance of hard work and completing a task. I learned about lasting commitment from him; I never feared my parents would divorce. My dad was absolutely committed to my mom. I felt secure and protected.

Most importantly, he taught me about character. He did what was right, even when no one was looking. I never heard him talk about cheating on taxes—he paid them and didn't grumble. His integrity was impeccable. I never heard him lie, and his eyes always demanded the same truth in return. The mental image of his character still fuels and energizes my life today.[3]

That's what we all want, isn't it? We want our children to see the Father's image in us. That means if you don't want your daughter to steal, you must be sure to pay the correct amount for your meal even when the waitress undercharges you. It means if you don't want your son to cheat, you must not try to take credit for a coworker's idea at the office, passing it off as your own. It means if you don't want your children to lie, you must tell the truth yourself, even when it's difficult, when it may be inconvenient, or when it may place you in a bad light. And you must do these things when your children are around and when they are not—for whether you are aware of it or not, they are watching you, much closer and much more often than you realize.

CULTIVATING VULNERABILITY AND TRANSPARENCY

My friend Norm Wakefield tells of a time when his son Joel was going through a hard time as a result of an unwise choice he had made. One day they went for a walk together, and Joel unloaded his woes on his dad. As they talked and walked together, Norm began to share an incident from his own experience in which he had faced a similar situation, responded unwisely, and experienced the consequences of that decision.

By sharing his own story, Norm helped Joel to see that although he did not condone his actions, he wasn't standing in ivory-towered judgment on his son. Norm's honesty and transparency with his son helped Joel see that his dad wanted to be his teammate and helper, not his judge. This encouraged him to open up further and allowed Norm to help his son think through the situation.

In fact, developing honesty in our kids requires honesty *in front of* our kids. The survey of churched kids which I cited earlier in this chapter revealed that 37 percent—more than one in three—say they seldom or never hear their parents admit to being wrong or having done wrong. It does little good to talk to our kids about being honest if we aren't willing to be honest ourselves. Believe me, I know how hard it is to admit to being wrong, but it is necessary if we want to raise kids who value honesty.

When my wife and I moved our family from California to Texas, our fifteen-year-old daughter struggled with the effects for quite a while afterward. One night, Katie made a comment that expressed her discontent. I got upset, said some cruel things, and came on pretty strong to her.

She went to her room and I went to bed. About fifteen minutes later, Dottie came in and woke me up.

"You need to go apologize to Katie," she said. "She was pretty hurt by what you said."

In my sleepiness (and pride), I said, "No, I'll take care of it in the morning."

"No," Dottie insisted, "you need to take care of it right now."

So I got dressed, went to my daughter's room, and apologized. I admitted to her that I had been wrong, that I didn't respond to her the way I should have, and I told her I was sorry. I believe that those moments of painful honesty with my daughter accomplished more for our relationship and for her understanding of honesty than anything else I may ever do.

When we blow it, we need to confess it honestly to God and to our children, make amends if possible, and walk on. Kids respect that. They'll remember it. They may even replicate it.

TEACHING HONESTY

As I was traveling across America speaking to churches as part of the "Right From Wrong" campaign, I called hundreds of high school or college students to join me on the platform. In front of the audience, I would ask the student, "Are you a Christian?" Most often, the young person would answer yes.

Then I'd ask, "Are your parents believers?" Again, most answered yes.

Then I'd say, "Let's suppose there's a situation where, if you lie, you could get out from under some painful circumstances. Would you lie?" I can't remember the last time somebody said that he or she wouldn't lie—right in front of the whole church!

I went to a major Bible college in Canada, thinking for sure the outcome would be different. But in front of 3,000 people, the guy said, "Yeah, I'd probably lie." (At least he was honest about his probable dishonesty!)

After the youth would make this revealing admission, I'd ask, "Have your parents taught you that lying is wrong?"

"Yes," they'd always say.

"Well," I'd continue, "how have they taught you that lying is wrong?"

Invariably, the answer would come back, "They tell me I shouldn't lie because the Bible says so— 'Thou shalt not lie.'"

Then I'd ask the most important question of the entire conversation: "And why does the Bible say you shouldn't lie?" I never had anyone give me an answer.

Do you see what has happened? Our kids know the precept— "Thou shalt not lie," for example—but that's *all* they know. They don't see the whole truth. They don't see that an all-important Person resides behind the precept. That's why I believe we must take advantage of every opportunity to impress upon our children the value of honesty, as well as the fact that honesty is right because God is true.

You may use the occasion of a television newscast or a car alarm going off in the neighborhood to discuss how the world would be different if everyone were honest and true, the way God is. (We wouldn't have to lock things up, chain things down, or install alarm systems, for example.) Such times can reinforce the understanding that God is a true God, full of truth, and that we honor him when we are honest.

You may also use shopping trips to reinforce God's standard of honesty. Let younger children pay the store cashier or insert the money in a vending machine. Then take a moment to briefly discuss why honesty is "the best policy." Guide older youth in a discussion of how stores must often compensate for shoplifting by raising prices and how that thwarts God's ideal.

ENCOURAGING HONESTY

When our children were still very young, my wife and I realized that we had been encouraging dishonesty in them by the way we responded to some situations.

If we walked into a room, for example, and saw one child and a broken lamp, we would invariably ask, "Did you break that lamp?" Or if we found one child crying and the other trying to talk her out of crying, we would almost always ask the child with the worried look, "Did you hit your sister?"

One day, we realized that confronting our children in this way made it very difficult for a young mind to answer truthfully. We could almost see the wheels turning in the child's mind: "I know the truthful answer to that question, but the truthful answer will get me in trouble. I'll try a lie and see if that works."

It seemed to us that by phrasing our questions as we did, we were encouraging dishonesty in our children. They felt almost trapped into lying. So we decided to give them a better chance to answer truthfully. We began asking (in a serious but not angry tone), "You broke that lamp, didn't you?" or "Why did you hit your sister?" Our former tactics promoted dishonesty; the new approach encouraged honesty.

We've since discovered other ways of encouraging honesty in our children. We've learned that moralizing, criticizing, and arguing are not the most effective approaches. We need to use restraint when tempted to relate to our children with a list of rules and regulations. Occasionally, our children need to feel our wrath at their persistent disobedience, but those times should be infrequent and balanced with abundant words that note our children's strengths and positive qualities.

REWARDING HONESTY

My earliest years as a father were not the most glorious. I assumed that a parent's job was to keep his children from sinning. I told myself, "If I spare the rod and spoil my children, that won't be pleasing to God." I wasn't abusive, but in those early years of fatherhood, I was almost always quick to pounce on them if they made mistakes, although I very rarely praised them for what they did right.

Suppose, for example, I was sitting in my study writing a book, and the words were really flowing. Dottie might come in and say, "Honey, Sean just came home with all A's on his report card."

"That's great," I'd probably reply. "I'm right in the middle of something right now. I'll talk to him about it at dinner."

At dinner, I might or might not remember to talk to him about his report card. But if Dottie had walked into my study and said, "Honey, Sean just punched Katie for going into his room," I would have jumped up from my desk and dealt with the problem immediately. Suddenly, my chapter wasn't as important. The matter couldn't wait until dinner. I had to deal with it now.

Today, as I talk to young people across the country, I estimate that fifteen out of twenty kids tell me that's exactly how it is at their house. They can get their parents' attention much faster if they do something wrong.

It wasn't until my oldest daughter was ten that I saw what I had been doing. I read a book called *The One Minute Manager*, in which the authors encourage business leaders to move around among their employees in an effort to "catch them doing something right" so they can offer appreciation and encouragement for their employees' efforts. That phrase turned things around for me, causing me to adopt a new motto as a father—"Try to catch your kids doing something right."

When I saw Sean taking out the trash, I would say, "Sean, thanks for remembering to take the trash out." When I caught Kelly doing homework, I would say, "Honey, I appreciate the way you study." When I entered a room to find Katie picking up her toys, I'd say, "Katie, I really appreciate how you take care of your things." This technique of trying to catch my kids doing something right mightily influenced my attitude toward my kids, and I think it reinforced positive behavior in them.

I especially tried to implement this practice in relation to honest attitudes and behaviors. I tried to catch my children being honest so I could reward them. It need not be a heroic display of honesty. It could simply have been paying a cashier the correct amount, admitting that a chore had been neglected, or repaying a debt promptly. I then dispensed hefty helpings of appreciation and occasional rewards, like a night of extended curfew or a one-time bonus in weekly allowance to say, "I value your honesty."

SHARING THE BENEFITS OF HONESTY

I also seized every opportunity to impress on my children the ways in which honesty and integrity protect us and provide for us. I tried to show them how God's standards of honesty, far from hurting them or holding them back in the world, can actually produce substantial benefits. I reminded them, for example, that the young man or woman who heeds God's standard of honesty will be protected from the burden of guilt. When you're honest, you don't always have to be looking over your shoulder.

I tried to impress upon them the fact that the young Christian who "speaks the truth" will reap the reward of "clean hands and a pure heart" toward God (Ps. 24:4).

I tried to help them see how a habit of honesty can protect a person from the embarrassment and shame that results when their deception is discovered.

I tried to help my children recognize that the reward for cheating is empty and short-lived, while the sense of accomplishment that comes with honest achievement is satisfying and lasting.

I also tried to help my kids see how God's standard of honesty provides a reputation for integrity. "A good name is more desirable than great riches," the Bible says; "to be esteemed is better than silver or gold" (Prov. 22:1).

I tried to help my children understand how God's standard of honesty protects and enriches relationships. The very foundation of relationships is built upon trust. Trust simply can't survive in the atmosphere of deceit. The element of trust is indispensable in building any successful, lifelong relationship. It undergirds marriage vows and business agreements with a reassuring, fortifying element. I wanted my kids to recognize that a strong foundation of trust will improve and enrich the quality of their relationships, providing something that money can't buy—and dishonesty can't achieve.

HELPING CHILDREN INTERNALIZE GOD'S STANDARD OF HONESTY

Helping our kids internalize God's standard of honesty is a priority for any father who seeks to reflect the image of God the Father. Our children may see godly values in our lives and hear us speak with conviction, but unless they internalize godly values themselves, they will still be vulnerable to compromise.

Our children may have the right answers but the wrong attitudes. Our goal should be to nurture internal motivation that will drive our children to honor Jesus Christ and to live responsible, productive, others-centered lives that flow out of a relationship with him, practicing obedience as a consequence of that relationship (John 14:21–24).

Internalizing values is a process. It begins with *information*. I spent a lot of time trying to impart information to my kids, teaching them about honesty, sharing the benefits of honesty.

But it doesn't stop there. *Interaction* with the truth is the next step in the process. I encouraged my son and daughters to test facts to see if they're valid, to see how they apply to various situations. This is where you, Dad, can be vitally involved by graciously, thoughtfully, and eagerly talking with your child. Question your children, encouraging *them* to question. Seek out new insights, new facts, new truth. Don't do this *for* your child but *with* him, leading him to form his convictions on solid foundations.

The third step, after imparting information and encouraging interaction with the truth, involves *implementing* the results of the information and interaction into their lifestyle. I tried to help my children follow through on what they'd been taught or had discovered for themselves through careful testing and experience. I might ask questions like, "What will that look like in your daily behavior?" or "Will that have any impact on how you drive or how you do your job or how you respond to your teachers?"

Again, this internalizing process involves: (1) imparting information; (2) interacting with the truth through investigation; and (3) acting on the truth in some tangible way. It's a process that is lifelong.

The formation of one's own values doesn't really begin until the early teenage years. Younger children simply don't have the mental maturity to process abstract ideas. But if Dad is modeling and teaching God's standard of honesty during the earlier years, children will stockpile those resources for future use. As children move into the teen years, the process of helping them internalize and personalize God's standards becomes more interactive.

One other important principle about internalization I'd like to share with you is this: our children's value system does not have to be an exact duplicate of our value system. We are not in the business of making clones of ourselves. Each child is a unique and separate person. They may have different ideas on certain subjects, feel more strongly on other issues, and perhaps just plain disagree with us at times yet still be following biblical guidelines in the values they adhere to. If their relationships with the Lord are solid, and if they are not going against a clear biblical standard, then allow them the freedom to think differently from you. Happy is the child whose parents also respect his values—or at least his right to have them.

The seven strategies discussed in this chapter—modeling honesty, cultivating both vulnerability and transparency, teaching honesty, encouraging honesty, rewarding honesty, sharing the benefits of honesty, and helping kids internalize God's standard of honesty—can go a long way (with God's help) toward enabling you to be the kind of father you want to be.

These strategies will help you raise children who become men and women of integrity, men and women whose reputations for honesty will win the respect and regard of others, children who learn the value of honest achievement as well as the emptiness of dishonest gain. They will help you raise children who avoid the consequences of dishonesty while helping you enjoy one of the greatest rewards of honesty—children who can be trusted.

They will help you raise children who reflect the image of their earthly father, as well as their heavenly Father.

For Reflection, Discussion, and Action

1. How might your children answer the questions that Josh asked Kelly on pages 57–58 in this chapter? Plan sometime this week to pose these questions to each of your children, guiding them to an understanding of God as the source of truth.

2. What are you doing to model a life of integrity to your children? Are there areas in which you have been less than honest? What do you need to change in those areas? Be specific.

_____
_____
_____
_____
_____
_____
_____
_____
_____
_____
_____
_____

*3. Select at least one suggestion from the section on "Teaching Honesty" to implement this week in an effort to impress or reinforce in your children the realization that honesty really is the best policy.

*4. Try to catch each of your kids doing something honest this week, then use it as an opportunity to express appreciation and to reward them for their honesty.

5. Complete these sentences:

I once paid the price of dishonesty when I _____

_____

_____

_____

I once reaped the benefits of honesty when I _____

_____

_____

_____

_____

Be prepared, if the opportunity presents itself, to honestly and openly share the experiences you listed above with your children as illustrations of the consequences of dishonesty and the benefits of honesty.

CHAPTER 6
The Trustworthy Father

The Steven Spielberg movie *Hook*, a contemporary retelling of the Peter Pan story, contains a scene that strikes a responsive chord in many children's hearts and minds.

Peter Banning, the character played by Robin Williams, is a successful businessman with many responsibilities. Peter gets an important phone call the evening before the family is to leave for a trip to England. So he schedules a crucial business meeting for the next morning, which also happens to be the morning of his son's final—and most important—baseball game of the season. His son Jack turns to him and reminds him of the game.

"I'll be there," his father says, insisting that the meeting will be short. "My word is my bond."

The next morning, as Peter's business meeting runs late, he dispatches an employee with a video camera, instructing him to go to his son's game and video "what I miss."

The employee arrives as Jack steps up to the plate for his final at-bat. The boy turns around to scan the bleachers for his dad, and instead sees the man with the video camera sitting beside his mother. A look of disappointment clouds Jack's face. He turns, faces the pitcher, and strikes out.

Peter arrives later at the park, screeching his car to a stop, and races up the hill to the rise overlooking the baseball diamond. The field is empty. Everyone has gone home.

Later that day, the family boards a plane bound for London, and while in flight Peter's daughter shows her father a picture.

"Look what Jack drew," she says, holding up a drawing of an airplane consumed in flames, diving toward the ocean. Four people are falling through the air beside the airplane. Only three are wearing parachutes.

Peter moves to the seat beside his son, who is bouncing a baseball off the overhead compartment above his seat.

"Why didn't I have a parachute, Jackie?" Peter asks.

"Take a wild guess," his son answers.

After a few moments, Peter says, "Jack, next season I'm coming to six games."

"Be sure you buy enough videotape," the boy responds bitterly.

"I promise," the father insists. "My word is my bond."

"Yeah," Jack answers. "Junk bond."

Those scenes are poignant because they are so terribly familiar to many fathers, sons, and daughters. How many fathers who love their children end up breaking promises, disappointing their children, embittering and exasperating them by making promises they don't keep? How many children have known the dashed hopes and terrible heartbreak caused by a father's broken promise?

That's not the kind of father I want to be. I want to keep my promises to my children. I want them to trust me, to be able to believe me when I tell them something, to see their father as a promise keeper, a man of his word, a man who does what he says he will do.

I want to be the kind of father my Father is.

The Trustworthy Father

God can be trusted to keep his promises. This may sound elementary, but it is fundamental to a healthy concept of God—and to a healthy concept of fatherhood. Our Father is the ultimate promise keeper. Faithfulness flows from his very nature:

> Because of the LORD's great love we are not consumed, for his compassions never fail. They are new every morning; great is your faithfulness. (Lam. 3:22–23)

> For no matter how many promises God has made, they are "Yes" in Christ. And so through him the "Amen" is spoken by us to the glory of God. (2 Cor. 1:20)

> Being confident of this, that he who began a good work in you will carry it on to completion until the day of Christ Jesus. (Phil. 1:6)

God fulfills every promise. The relationship we have with the Father rests on faith and trust. King David, who spent much of his life facing enemies and fighting battles, knew where to place his trust. "Some trust in chariots," he wrote, "and some in horses, but we trust in the name of the LORD our God" (Ps. 20:7). David knew that his Father was reliable, dependable. He knew that what his Father said, his Father would do.

We, like David, can trust God because he is always trustworthy and faithful. Even when we break our promises to him, he still loves us and keeps his promises to us. "If we are faithless, he will remain faithful, for he cannot disown himself" (2 Tim. 2:13). In other words, faithfulness and trustworthiness are an intrinsic part of God's nature. He cannot be otherwise because that would contradict who he is. It would be like disowning himself.

That's the kind of father I want to be—the kind of father who keeps his promises, who invites the trust of his children and rewards their trust. I want to be the kind of father who does what he says he will do, and whose children become reliable and dependable because of his influence on them.

That's asking a lot, I know. I also know that I am not equal to the task. But my Father is. And the more I depend on him and walk with him day by day, the more I become like him in the following ways:

TAKING PROMISES SERIOUSLY

Many of us make mistakes and break promises as fathers because we don't recognize how serious our promises to our children are. We don't see the momentous effect that broken promises (and kept promises) have on our children.

Dr. James L. Schaller, in his book *The Search for Lost Fathering*, tells of a man who spent an entire day fishing with his son. That night, the father—an influential man, a wielder of power in the nation's corridors—recorded in his diary, "Today, I went fishing with my son. A day wasted."

His son also kept a diary, where he recorded his own reflections on his return home that evening. *His* notation for that day differed considerably from his father's. It read, "Went fishing with my father today—the greatest day of my life."[1]

This father apparently had no idea of the true power he held in his hands, because he could not see things from his son's perspective. I've learned that when I begin to see things through the eyes of my children, I begin to appreciate the importance of my promises. When I begin to see through my children's eyes, I see how a broken promise looks to them. It looks like: "Dad's got more important things to worry about." "Dad's not interested in what I'm doing." "I'm not very important." "I'm not very good."

From that perspective, it's not hard to see how important my promises are and how seriously I need to take them.

KEEPING PROMISES TO OUR CHILDREN

It's easy to say we should keep our promises to our kids. We all want to do that. We know we should. But it's quite another thing to follow through.

I realized long ago that as I look at my life, I judge myself based on my intentions. But that doesn't necessarily get the job done. As someone has observed, the road to a very hot, unpleasant place of biblical proportions is paved with "good intentions."

My children, however, judge me not on my intentions but on my actions, on how I *follow through* on my intentions. It doesn't matter too much to them that I *intend* to spend time with my kids if I don't follow through on that intention. It doesn't matter too much to them that I *intend* to keep my promises to them if I don't follow through on that intention.

One of the things that has helped me in this area of keeping promises to my children is realizing that I make two kinds of promises to my kids: *implicit* and *explicit*. Both are extremely important. And the more I can take implicit promises and make them explicit, the more I help myself and my kids.

For example, some of the implicit promises that come with being a father are to love our children, to protect them from harm, to provide for their physical needs, and to supply the knowledge and guidance they need to become healthy adults. In most families, those promises are assumed and implied.

I have tried, however, to take those implicit promises and make them explicit.[2] Yes, I told my children that I would do those things for them, but I added other explicit promises like, "I promise to put you ahead of my work" and "I promise to listen anytime you have a problem you need to talk about."

But in striving to make implicit promises more explicit, I have learned a lot about the promises my kids expect me to keep. I've learned, for example, that in their minds, a promise to protect them from harm includes not denigrating them or complaining about them to other people, which is a fair expectation—a promise I intend to keep. I've also had the opportunity to clarify my promises for my children. I explained, for example, that my promise to provide for their physical needs did not necessarily mean I would make sure they kept pace with every changing style and compete with their friends' wardrobes.

A father who clarifies his promises to his children and commits himself to consistently keeping those promises will give his children a priceless gift—a father who is dependable, reliable, and trustworthy.

KEEPING PROMISES TO GOD

Children will learn two things (among many others) by watching a father's relationship with God. They will learn whether *God* can be trusted and whether *Dad* can be trusted.

If my children see me placing my trust in my bank account, or good works, or anything other than God who keeps his promises, they may conclude that God can't be trusted. Conversely, if they see me placing myself and my family in God's care, leaning on his strength, trusting in his care, and believing in his promises, they will more likely come to know God as a faithful God.

My children may also pick up clues from my relationship with God as to whether *I* can be trusted. If they observe me treating my promises to God lightly, or breaking my vows to him, they may be led to doubt my trustworthiness. If I routinely make and break promises to God, my children may come to expect no better in my relationships with them. The result, of course, will be an erosion of trust between me and my children.

That's not what I want, of course, and I imagine it's not what you want either. I want my children to see me keeping my promises to God by his grace and power:

How can I repay the Lord for all his goodness to me?. . . I will fulfill my vows to the Lord in the presence of all his people. (Ps. 116:12, 14)

I want to fulfill my vows to the Lord in the presence of all his people . . . including my own children.

KEEPING PROMISES TO OTHERS

A friend of mine shared an experience with his fifth-grade son, Jordan, that has reminded me of the importance of keeping my promises to others.

Two of Jordan's closest buddies were simultaneously struggling through their parents' divorce at this particular time. And one evening after Jordan had gone to bed, his parents engaged in a heated "discussion" that he could hear from his bedroom. These parents had been careful over the years not to have angry confrontations in front of their children, but they were unaware that Jordan was still awake and able to hear everything. In the midst of the argument, the mother finally turned and noticed her son quietly sitting in the doorway of their bedroom with tears streaming down his face.

Mom and Dad instantly stopped their argument. The father picked up his son and asked, "Jordan, were you having a nightmare?"

Jordan sobbed heavily, managing to ask through his sobs, "Daddy, when are you and Mom going to get your divorce?"

"Whatever made you think we might get a divorce?" the father asked.

"John and James say their parents fight a lot," he said, fear etched on his face, "and now you and Mom are fighting."

At that moment, both parents quickly sobered. Their anger evaporated. And they used that "teaching moment" to tell Jordan how important their marriage was. They told him that they loved each other, that they had made promises to each other when they got married, and that they intended to keep those promises.

A father who breaks his promises to his wife, his friends, or his business associates will find it difficult to build trust in a son or daughter. But a dad who keeps his promises to others will encourage and enlarge a spirit of trust among his children, as well.

BECOMING ACCOUNTABLE

I surprise many parents when I advise them to become accountable to their own kids.

Most parents consider my suggestion slightly radical, perhaps even subversive. They look at me like I've just stuck out my tongue at them and wiggled my fingers in my ears. After all, kids are supposed to be accountable to *parents*, not vice versa. But I sincerely believe that becoming accountable to our kids is one of the most effective ways of keeping our promises and building trust between father and child. I'm not suggesting, now, that you put your children in charge—far from it! What I do suggest, however, is being humble and submissive enough to give your children permission to call you to account when you break a promise.

When Kelly turned seven, I put a special note in her birthday card that read:

> Dear Kelly, I sure love you. I count it such a joy to be your dad, but you know, I'm going to need your help this year. I've never been the father of a seven-year-old daughter before. I just want to be the best dad I can be to you. And if you ever feel that I'm not doing right or being fair, or loving and considerate, please tell me.

I've done the same with Sean and Katie and Heather, in turn. I have tried to become accountable to each of my four children. I have enlisted their participation in helping me keep my promises to them, and as a result, they have become four of my most valued counselors.

Of course, being accountable to your children can get uncomfortable. When my daughter Katie was ten years old, she confronted me upon my return from a trip.

"Daddy," she said, "you're not being fair to me."

Now, one of the promises to my children I try to keep is to be fair with them. So I answered, "What do you mean, honey?"

"When you come home from trips," she said, "you take Kelly and Sean and Heather out, but not me."

"Really?" I said. This came as a complete surprise to me.

"Yes," she said unflinchingly. Then her expression softened, and she asked, "Will you take me out for lunch today?"

Well, you can be sure I had lunch with my ten-year-old daughter that day. The effect of my willingness to be accountable to my daughter was found in helping me realize—and correct—a mistake I was making.

That's the point of accountability. Keeping our promises to our kids is a tough job. (If it were easy, more of us would do it, wouldn't we?) It's a job that requires God's help, certainly. It's also a job our kids can help us with. And, believe me, if they're given that opportunity and responsibility, they will!

The ideas above will not only help you be the kind of father who invites the trust of his children and who does what he says he will do. They will also help you become the father of children who can be trusted, children who are reliable and dependable because of your influence. Through your reliance on God's Holy Spirit and the faithful implementation of the above ideas, your children can become promise keepers themselves—men and women whose word can be trusted, whose promises can be believed.

For Reflection, Discussion, and Action

1. When was the last time you broke a promise to one of your children? (If you can't recall, ask your kids!) What do you think this broken promise communicated to your child? (Again, if you don't know, ask the child!)

2. Use the space below (or a separate sheet of paper) to list any implied promises you have made to your children:

_____

_____

_____

_____

_____

3. Which of the above implicit promises should you make explicit? Circle all that apply.

*4. Use the space below (or a separate sheet of paper) to list explicit promises you have made to your children:

_____

_____

_____

_____

_____

*5. Make plans to become accountable to your children this week. How will you do that? (Talk to each child individually, sit them down in a group and talk to them, write them notes giving them permission to help you keep your promises.)

CHAPTER 7
The Father Who Comforts and Supports

Fourteen-year-old Amy vividly remembers the first time it happened. She was five years old.

A thunderstorm outside her bedroom window woke her up in the middle of the night. Frightened of the dark and of the roaring thunder outside, she leaped from her bed and ran crying into her parents' bedroom.

She padded to the side of her parents' bed and cried softly for her mother. Before her mother could respond, however, her father awoke.

"What are you doing out of bed?" he said, angry at having been awakened. "Get back in your own room."

"But, Daddy, I'm scared," she answered, crying harder.

"I don't want to hear it. You're a big girl, and it's time you start acting like one." Amy shot a pleading glance at her mother, who sat up in bed, but her mother only stared at the floor.

"Did you hear me?" her father shouted, causing Amy to jump. "I said 'get back to bed.' And don't bother us again."

Amy left her parents' bedroom and walked to the bathroom. She turned on the light, locked the door behind her, and spent the rest of the night in the tub, crying, shuddering at every crack of thunder.

This same scene was repeated several times before Amy learned not to expect comfort from her father. Until the age of ten, she spent stormy nights crying in the bathtub, with the lights on and the door locked.

The worst thing about Amy's story is that it's true. She has since gotten over her fear of thunderstorms, but she still suffers the results of the lack of comfort and support she received from her father.

The result of these types of experiences can be devastating. According to Dr. David Ferguson and Dr. Don McMinn of the Center for Marriage and Family Intimacy, a person whose need for comfort and support is not being met is likely to feel discouraged, alone, empty, and timid. Such a person is more prone to promiscuity, fear of failure, weariness toward life, and obsessive-compulsive orientation.

A young person who doesn't experience a father's comfort and support will find it more difficult to handle feelings of insecurity and withstand unhealthy peer pressure. A young person who doesn't experience a father's comfort and support may experience trouble forming healthy friendships, and will more likely succumb to the pressure of becoming sexually active in an effort to meet those emotional needs.

On the positive side, a young person who *does* receive a father's comfort and support is more likely to feel loved, grateful, and hopeful—to be caring, compassionate, positive, giving, sensitive, and self-confident themselves.[1]

As much as I deplore the conduct of Amy's father, I must admit there have been times when I have failed to offer the comfort and support my children need. But that's not the father you or I want to be. We want to be the kind of fathers who are there when our children need comfort and support, who respond sensitively to a child's fears and hurts. We want to be the kind of fathers who by their comfort and support equip their children to stand up to

unhealthy peer pressure, battle insecurity, build healthy friendships, and earn the respect and admiration of their peers.

We want to be the kind of father our Father is.

The Father Figure

The nature and character of our Father in heaven reveals
that a godly father is one who comforts and supports his children
in life's trials and difficulties. "The righteous cry out," the Bible
says, "and the LORD hears them; he delivers them from all their
troubles. The LORD is close to the brokenhearted and saves those
who are crushed in spirit" (Ps. 34:17–18).

He is "the Father of compassion and the God of all comfort,
who comforts us in all our troubles, so that we can comfort those
in any trouble with the comfort we ourselves have received from
God" (2 Cor. 1:3–4).

Our Model Father is the Father of compassion and the God
of all comfort. He responds to our crises and calamities, not with
impatience and indignation but with comfort and support. He
knows that it helps immensely in times of difficulty to have someone on whom we can rely, someone in whom we can find strength,
someone from whom we can gain wise counsel.

God's comfort extends to "all our troubles." He comforts and
supports us when we suffer persecution for his name's sake and
when we suffer the consequences of our own stupid behavior. He
comforts us when we deserve it least, when we're slogging through
a mess of our own making. He supports us when we are weak, and
he comforts us when we fall.

> He tends his flock like a shepherd: He gathers the lambs
> in his arms and carries them close to his heart; he gently
> leads those that have young. (Isa. 40:11)

Our Father is comforting and supporting even when he must
discipline us. The psalmist David wrote, "Your rod and your staff,
they comfort me" (Ps. 23:4). The shepherd's staff was used as an

instrument of comfort and support, lifting newborns, drawing lambs closer, and guiding sheep through dangerous or difficult routes. The rod, on the other hand, was an instrument of defense and discipline. It was used to deter or subdue attackers and for correcting wayward or recalcitrant members of the flock.[2] Both instruments, however—the staff *and* the rod—were sources of comfort to the psalmist, because both were wielded by a compassionate and supportive Shepherd.

That's the kind of father we should want to be. By the supernatural presence and power of God's Holy Spirit living in us and working through us, we can reflect our Father's nature, comforting and supporting our children in all their troubles.

It was easy, of course, to comfort my daughter when she came home from school disappointed because she got a B on a test instead of an A. It was easy to support my son when he had a less than stellar game on the soccer field. It's easy to comfort a child who's just fallen off a bike or broken off an engagement. But it's not so easy to offer comfort and support when they wreck the car because of a silly stunt, when they fail a test because they haven't studied, when they put off responsibilities to the last minute and then mess up. Those kinds of struggles—the ones they bring upon themselves—make it more difficult to respond in a godly way. But it is precisely at those times that our children most need to feel our comfort and support.

We still tend to come on too strong to our kids. We resort too quickly to yelling, lecturing, and scolding at times. But we can learn. We can learn how to show the image of our Father by comforting and supporting our children, learning new ways to conform to his likeness, new techniques that foster the Father's image in our own fathering, such as:

ACCEPTING YOUR LIMITATIONS

Bob, a young father, once told me about his efforts to help his six-year-old daughter learn to ride a bicycle. Bob ran alongside Heather's bike to stabilize her while she learned to coordinate the many actions involved in riding a bike: steering, pedaling, braking, balancing. In the process, however, Bob accidentally let go of the bike. It crashed, sending Heather tumbling to the ground in a heap.

As he related the incident, Bob expressed his dismay at having "failed" his daughter. He really wanted Heather to trust that he would be there, to believe that she could depend on him to support her, not only in that specific task but in everything.

But Bob wasn't perfect. None of us are.

One of the keys to becoming fathers who comfort and support their children is understanding and accepting our limitations. We can't prevent our kids from skinning their knees, but we can be there to pick them up and kiss their hurts. We can't stop our kids from making mistakes, but we can be there to help them *correct* their mistakes. We can't protect our kids from disappointment and harm, but we can be there to cry and hurt with them. We can't fix everything that goes wrong in their lives, but we can cheer them on when they succeed and lift them up when they fail.

We can't do everything for our kids. But if with God's help we do what we can, it will be enough.

TAKING TIME

One of the respondents to our "Why Wait?" survey wrote an essay about her first sexual activity. The essay read, in part:

> I had a rotten day at school, and all I wanted was a little bit of my parents' time. Just a simple hug would do. But they were too busy, so I went to my boyfriend with my problems. One thing led to another and now I'm involved sexually. Dad, Mom, I wish you had been there when I needed you.

That young woman needed comfort after a difficult day at school, and she sought it first from her parents. But when her parents were too busy, she sought it elsewhere.

As I've said before, kids don't spell love the same way adults do. They spell it T-I-M-E. A father who truly wants to reflect the image of the Father of compassion, the God of all comfort, must take time for his children.

I certainly wasn't always a paragon of virtue in this area. Once, when I was in the middle of writing a book at our favorite vacation retreat in Mexico, Kelly walked in and said, "Daddy, would you take me to get my nails done?"

I was on a roll, and my first thought was, "This is the last thing I need right now."

My second thought was, "Josh, practice what you preach."

My third thought was, "Lord, give me the right attitude about this."

Well, I put my work away and took my daughter to get her nails done, hoping that later I could again catch the "wave" I had been riding at that moment in my writing. Happily (my wife might say "surprisingly"), I recognized that it wasn't just a matter of being Kelly's personal taxi driver to get her somewhere. What she really wanted was my time. And as it turned out, we had a great time together and a meaningful talk on the way back. In fact, the most intimate and heartfelt subjects Kelly shared with me didn't come up until near the end of our journey that day. It took time for Kelly to open up, and I'm glad it was time I was able and willing to give her.

Kelly must have thanked me three or four times for taking her to get her nails done. I think that's because by taking time for her, I not only communicated my interest in her, but also because I placed myself in a position to offer comfort and support to her.

GAUGING THEIR NEEDS

My friend Norm Wakefield tells of an occasion when one of his daughters was approaching her high school graduation, a time when a parent would expect a teen to be happy and hopeful. But Norm observed that his daughter was subdued and quiet. A conversation with her revealed that she felt discouraged because many of her classmates would be receiving special awards and scholarships at graduation, while she didn't expect to receive any special recognition at all.

Norm could have done many things. He could have dismissed her feelings. He could have told her she was being silly. He could have tried to reason with her. But he recognized that none of those responses would have met her need at that moment.

"I didn't know what to say," he says now, but he put his arm around her, squeezed her, and said, "In my book, you're number one." His daughter's smile and hug told him that he hadn't done too badly for a dad who didn't know what to say. His estimation of her need was accurate. She needed comfort. She needed to hear that whether or not she got any awards or scholarships, there was someone who held her in high esteem.

A father who wishes to offer comfort and support to his children needs to be sensitive to their needs. Listen closely to what they say. Observe what they do. But don't stop there. Try to gauge what feelings and needs those words and actions reflect. A child who says, "You never do anything with me" may be expressing a need for a father's attention. A child who looks to the bleachers before stepping up to home plate may be looking for support. A child who throws a temper tantrum when she fails may be crying out for comfort.

I'm not saying we need to excuse inappropriate behavior. I *am* suggesting we should notice—even anticipate—our children's needs, and respond not only to their words and actions but also to the needs that prompt them.

LEARNING THE LANGUAGE OF COMFORT AND SUPPORT

There are certain things a kid does *not* need when he or she is afraid or embarrassed or disappointed or hurting. Since I usually take a generally cognitive approach to problems (and to people), my first instinct toward someone who's hurting is rational ("You know, your mistake was. . ." or "You know why this happened, don't you?"). I'm learning, however, that hurting people seldom need correction ("Let this be a lesson to you"), nor do they need instruction ("This can really build your character, if you let it"), advice ("If I were you . . ."), or inspiration ("Cheer up! It could be a lot worse, you know").

Instead of following my first instinct, I've learned instead that more often than not, my kids need me to be there with them, to hug them, to cry with them, to hold their hands, to hurt with them, and to show them that I care. I've learned that they seldom need my correction and they seldom profit from my advice. They don't need a sermon; they need a shoulder to cry on. They need comfort and support. And this is often best expressed through the language of comfort ("I'm sorry, honey," "I know it hurts," "I'm here," "I love you") and the language of support ("I believe in you," "We can get through this together," and "I'll be right there the whole time").

Sometimes, of course, it's quite necessary to offer discipline or correction when a young person is suffering the consequences of their own misconduct, but discipline will be much more effective when a father has first offered comfort and support.

WATCHING YOUR MOUTH

Dan Benson, in his book *The Total Man*, tells how one survey of parents revealed that moms and dads average ten negative comments to their kids for every one positive comment. Yet he observes, "Experts in child psychology believe that it takes at least four positive remarks to offset the damage to self-esteem caused by one negative comment."[3]

The father who hopes to communicate comfort and support to his kids must be aware of the power of his words to help or hurt. If he is consistently sarcastic, condemning, or critical with his words, any effort to comfort and support his children will be ineffective. If his verbal and nonverbal language is saying, "Get away from me," "Don't bother me," "I prefer the companionship of adults," "I don't have time for you," "I think you're stupid," "I don't particularly like you," "You're a nuisance," "I won't consider your views or feelings," he will alienate himself from his children and force them to search elsewhere for the comfort and support they need.

ENTERING THEIR WORLD

If you really want your kids to feel your comfort and support, try entering their world. Make it your mission to discover what they're interested in right now, what they think is cool, what they enjoy, what kind of friends they're hanging around with.

Many of us dads expect our kids to communicate with us on our level. We expect them to do things that interest *us*, yet we seldom or never enter into their interests and communicate at their level.

Some years ago, my daughter Kelly had a friend over, and they started pestering me about "doing" my hair.

"Oh, you don't really want to do my hair," I insisted.

"Come on, Dad," Kelly pleaded.

I really didn't want those two girls playing guinea pig with me, but I saw the opportunity to enter into their world.

"Okay," I said at last. "You can do my hair any way you want to, but you can't cut it or dye it and you both have to agree to go out to dinner with me afterward."

"All right!" they shrieked in unison. And for the next hour or so, they went at it with mousse, hair dryer, and a few other tools I didn't recognize. When they finished, they had my hair sticking out in every direction. I looked like a flying saucer, ready to take off for a distant planet. As I gazed in the mirror, I thought twice about the other end of the deal. Did I really want to go out to dinner in public? I could only hope no one would recognize me.

When we walked into the local pizza parlor (dark glasses and all), the girls stayed about five feet behind me because they didn't want anyone to know they were with me. People did stare, and one woman rolled her eyes repeatedly, but at least no one called the police. And we had a hilarious time.

Now, I don't think this experience was particularly comforting or supporting for my daughter. But along with other things like dates, water balloon fights, popcorn parties in the jacuzzi, and similar moments, it taught me many things about my children that enabled me to offer comfort and support when they needed it. By entering their world as often as possible, I learned to read their moods, understand their feelings, and anticipate their struggles in ways I could not have done otherwise.

The ability to offer comfort and support is not like a television, something you simply turn on when it's needed. It's more like a garden. It requires constant cultivation and care so that when the time comes—at unpredictable moments—the fruit of your labors can be reaped.

Offering comfort and support to your children will have a long-reaching effect, both on them and on you. You'll be able to watch them stand up to unhealthy peer pressure, confident that they can find ample support and comfort when needed in their own home. You'll see them develop healthy friendships in which they are able not only to receive but to give as well. You will observe them—more and more as they grow—earning the respect and admiration of their peers (and of yours) as they become capable, confident young men and women who know that whatever else may happen at school, work, or church, they can find comfort and support in their father.

For Reflection, Discussion, and Action

1. Review the following list and consider whether your children reflect any of these characteristics (check any that apply):

   ❑ discouraged
   ❑ timid
   ❑ afraid of failure
   ❑ insecure
   ❑ vulnerable to peer pressure
   ❑ forms unhealthy friendships

   ❑ alone
   ❑ promiscuous
   ❑ obsessive-compulsive
   ❑ empty
   ❑ vulnerable to sexual pressure
   ❑ weary toward life

2. If you checked any of the characteristics above, do you think any of those feelings or difficulties might be related to a lack of comfort and support from you? If so, which ones?

3. Can you identify any times in the past when you have failed to offer comfort and support to a child who needed it? Is it possible to correct that failure? Do you need to ask forgiveness of that child?

*4. In the space provided below, make a list of the ways you can begin offering comfort and support to your children. Then identify one step you will take this week by circling it.

_____

_____

_____

*5. Think ahead to events that are coming up in your children's lives. At what times do you think they might most need your comfort and support? What can you do now to anticipate and prepare for those moments?

CHAPTER 8
The Father as Refuge

Denise, the daughter of a good friend of mine, once had a run-in with one of her high school teachers. The teacher had accused Denise of something she had not done, and despite the lack of any evidence, had threatened to severely penalize Denise with detentions or suspension. Denise repeatedly pleaded her innocence, yet the teacher persisted in her determination to mete out punishment. But Denise stood her ground.

"I want to call my dad," she insisted, hurt and afraid.

"We'll just have to do that, now, won't we?" said the teacher, apparently assuming that Denise's father would be embarrassed and angered by his daughter's supposed guilt.

The teacher then marched Denise to the school office and stood beside the phone as Denise called her father to explain the situation.

"He's coming," Denise said, on the verge of tears as she hung up the telephone.

Within just a few minutes, Denise's dad arrived at the school and sat down with his daughter and her teacher. Having briefly heard Denise's story over the phone, he asked the teacher to explain the problem. She did so, angrily and defensively.

Finally, Denise's dad stood. "I've heard enough," he said. He placed his arm around his daughter, and then politely informed the teacher that she had accused the wrong person, and that he would not tolerate any detention, suspension, or retaliation of any kind against his daughter. He walked out of the office with Denise in his arms, asking his daughter to wait there while he concluded the meeting with the teacher.

He returned to the office and explained to the teacher why he was certain of Denise's innocence, and told the teacher that he thought his daughter was owed an apology. Then he turned once more to leave. When he reached the hallway again, his daughter was again close to tears.

"What's wrong?" he said, confused because the crisis seemed to be past.

Barely holding back the tears, Denise smiled and threw her arms around her father's neck. "Thanks, Dad, for being there for me," she said. "You're my defender."

That father communicated something extremely valuable to his daughter that day. It may have seemed rather routine at that time, but he earned his daughter's gratitude by being a refuge for her. That incident created (or enhanced) a sense of safety and security in her mind that said, "I can rely on Dad. I can run to him when I'm in trouble. He will defend me. He will be my advocate."

Fostering that kind of attitude in a child is particularly crucial for today's dads. A majority of today's young people view the future of society with apprehension. Many seem to have lost hope in their own future. They walk the corridors of fear and anxiety. Six in ten high school students say they know a peer who has attempted or committed suicide,[1] and one in three knows someone who has brought a weapon to school.[2] Many have friends or acquaintances who are involved in dangerous or illegal behavior, such as premarital sex and drug abuse. Other research shows that 68 percent of younger teens do not believe that this world even *has* a future, and 32 percent believe they will be directly affected by nuclear annihilation. Such fears extend even to younger children. Several years ago, Nadine Brozan reported in *The New York Times* the results of a study that found the five greatest fears of a primary-school child thirty years ago: loud noises, dark rooms, high places, dangerous animals, and strangers. Today, the average primary child's greatest fears look more like this: losing a parent through divorce, being a victim of burglary, muggings, rape, or cancer.[3] Add to this the fear of terrorism, and our kids have a whole different world to deal with than we or our parents did.

Kids need a safe place in such a climate, a place of refuge and retreat from the dangers and disappointments of a world gone mad. They need shelter from the storm. They need a place to lick their wounds, a place to find relief.

That's what I want to be for my kids. I want to be the kind of father my Father is.

A Father, A Fortress

At the lowest point in his life, having been pursued and persecuted by the king (the father of his best friend), a former shepherd boy named David lived in hiding. He had been a national hero; now he was in exile. He had been a member of the king's court; now he slept in caves. He had served his king loyally; now the king's counselors defamed David to the king. He had been anointed as the next king of Israel; now his future seemed dark. He had mercifully spared the king's life; now that same king *sought* his life.

David's problems loomed so large that he felt like a man among lions, trembling like a child among ravenous beasts. He felt bowed down, doubled over with the burden of his trouble. Finally, in his distress, David turned to his Father, his God. He cried out:

Have mercy on me, O God, have mercy on me, for in you my soul takes refuge. I will take refuge in the shadow of your wings until the disaster has passed. (Ps. 57:1)

Within a few years, however, David became king, defeated all his enemies, united a kingdom in turmoil, and won the respect and regard of his people. How were such things accomplished? David provides the answer in a later psalm:

I love you, O LORD, my strength. The LORD is my rock, my fortress and my deliverer; my God is my rock, in whom I take refuge. He is my shield and the horn of my salvation, my stronghold. (Ps. 18:1–2)

That's the kind of Father our God is! He is our defense, our strong tower, our refuge, our hiding place:

The Lord is a refuge for the oppressed, a stronghold in times of trouble. (Ps. 9:9)

The Lord Almighty is with us; the God of Jacob is our fortress. (Ps. 46:7)

He is my loving God and my fortress, my stronghold and my deliverer, my shield, in whom I take refuge, who subdues peoples under me. (Ps. 144:2)

Both high and low among men find refuge in the shadow of your wings. (Ps. 36:7)

Our Model Father is a source of strength, a safe place to his children. In him we can find safety from the attacks and pressures of the world. God is a refuge.

Isn't that the kind of father you want to be? Oh, you can't be as almighty or all-knowing as he is. You want them to turn first and foremost to their heavenly Father. Just as he is *your* fortress and refuge, you want him to be their refuge as well. We all do.

But I know you want to be like him. You want to be a refuge for your children. You want them to know that there is always a safe place they can run to—wherever Daddy is. You want them to know that they can come to you for refuge from the storms of life, from the attacks of their peers, from the pressures of adolescence, from disappointment and ridicule and fear. If they know that refuge and safety are available in Dad, they are more likely to feel safe and secure, not only in your home and family but in themselves. They will be more apt to develop self-esteem and self-confidence if they know that someone is behind them, willing to speak up for them, willing to shelter and support them.

Like everything else, this is an impossible task if you try to achieve it in your own strength and wisdom. On your own, you would certainly blow it every time. But you're not on your own. You "can do everything through him who gives [you] strength" (Phil. 4:13). And as you rely on God the Father through his Holy Spirit, he will work through you to perform a few sound strategies, such as the following:

PREPARING FOR CRISIS

I picked up my daughter Kelly from school one day. As we walked across the parking lot to the car, she suddenly asked, "Daddy, what do you think of Jim Bakker?"

At that time, televangelists Jim and Tammy Bakker had been all over the news, and the scandal that destroyed their PTL television empire had become discussion material for my daughter's junior high classroom.

I had already heard many pastors and other Christians react to the PTL scandal, saying such things as, "It's disgusting," "They ought to be thrown out of the ministry," "He's probably not even a real Christian" and so on. I understood the sense of disappointment and outrage such statements expressed, but I also realized something else. I was painfully aware that any pastor saying such things about Jim Bakker also took the risk of communicating to the young people in his church, "If you ever get into trouble, don't come to me." To all the teen girls in the congregation, his tone was saying, "If you get pregnant out of wedlock, I'll condemn you without batting an eye." Christian parents who spoke about Jim Bakker in such terms risked communicating to their own kids, "We'll be there for you as long as you don't get on drugs, don't drink, don't get pregnant, don't get into trouble."

So how could I answer Kelly's question? How could I walk the line between telling my thirteen-year-old daughter what I thought of sin without condemning the sinner?

I swallowed hard, bit my lip, and said, "Honey, what Jim Bakker did was wrong. It was sin." I went on to explain why it was sin for Jim Bakker to do some of the things he had done. And then I said, "But Kelly, I want you to realize something. God loves Jim Bakker as much as he loves you or me. And Christ died for him as much as he died for you and me. If God can't forgive Jim Bakker, then he can't forgive you or me."

As we continued walking across the parking lot toward the car, Kelly said nothing for a few moments, while my head was spinning with all I wanted to say to my daughter. Finally, I took a deep breath and said, "Honey, let's look at this realistically. If you got pregnant, can you imagine what your dad would go through? I'd get crucified. Half the people here in our own church would turn on me. All over the country, Christian leaders, magazine editors, reporters, evangelists—they'd all have me for lunch."

Kelly looked up at me, her blue eyes wide with concern. "I know it, Dad," she said.

"But honey, I want you to know one thing," I said. "If you ever did get pregnant, I wouldn't care what all those people would say. I'd turn my back on all that, but I'd never turn my back on you. I'd put my arms around you and we'd see it through together."

At that moment, my thirteen-year-old daughter dropped her books, right on the parking lot pavement, started crying, threw her arms around me and said, "I know you would, Daddy!"

Now, some people might think I was taking too big a risk, that Kelly might think, "Dad will love me anyway, so it doesn't matter if I get pregnant." But I didn't worry so much about that, because I wanted to be her refuge, not only if she got pregnant but when she got into trouble of any kind. I wanted her—and her brother and sisters—to know that I will be their defender, their safe place, their shelter in the storm.

BEING ALERT AND OBSERVANT

In a book that my friend Norm Wakefield and I wrote together, he told of the importance of being alert:

My son Joel (at that time an eighth-grader) came home from school in an irritable mood. I was in my den and heard him slamming doors and speaking rudely. At the dinner table he was cranky and sarcastic. Later in the evening, I was in my den and again heard him angrily slam the door to his bedroom.

Finally the glaring light went on in my mind: something important must be bothering Joel. For the past four hours he had been visibly upset. I went to his room and said, "Joel, I just realized that you came home in an irritable mood. Is there something that happened at school you'd like to talk about?"

My son began to weep (and frankly, I felt like a dummy for not seeing the problem sooner). He poured out his hurt concerning an incident that had happened in the classroom. He had been embarrassed and misunderstood by a teacher. Not knowing how to process it, he carried it home and it kept leaking out in his negative behavior. . . . I'm thankful the message got through to me."

Being a refuge requires a father to be alert and observant. It will mean being sensitive to your children's words and moods. It will mean respecting their worries and concerns. It will mean getting to know their friends. It may mean watching some of the television shows they watch, and even (yikes!) listening to some of their music.

One father I know, who works at home, makes it a habit to greet his kids the moment they walk in the door from school. They then come into his office, one at a time, to sit on his lap (they're teenagers!) and tell him about their day at school. This routine usually takes no more than fifteen minutes out of his workday, but it allows him to touch base with his kids. It lets them unload their concerns or celebrate their joys with their dad at the end of a school day.

That technique may not work for you. But find something that does work, something that keeps you alert and helps you be sensitive to your children and what they're going through.

LEARNING TO LISTEN

A successful businessman, unhappy about his relationship with his eighteen-year-old son, came to Norm for counseling. The father explained that his son was unmotivated, involved in drugs, and had established destructive relationships. Communication between father and son had become strained, almost to the breaking point.

Norm suggested that the father take his son to lunch the following week—"not to chastise or preach to him," Norm explained. "Your task is to express an interest in him. To listen."

When the businessman returned the following week, he described the event.

"How did your son respond?" Norm asked.

"Well," the dad began, "he said that all during the lunch time he kept waiting for the shoe to drop!" The son had expected his dad to correct or reprimand him, because that was what had happened all the other times they had talked. It surprised the son that his father would be willing to simply listen to him!

Fathers who truly want to become a refuge to their children must develop and refine the art of listening. Too often, our children come to us in tears, in distress, in trouble, and as soon as they've revealed the problem, we fathers are ready with correction, reprimand, instruction, or advice:

"Haven't I tried to tell you . . . ?"

"What were you thinking?"

"I can't believe you could do such a stupid thing!"

"This is the last straw!"

"Okay, here's what you have to do now. . . ."

But if we have made the Father Connection and are prayerfully seeking to reflect his image in our parenting, we will take time to listen first, to hear the whole story, to withhold criticism or condemnation, letting our children pour out their troubles without fear that we will jump to conclusions or rush to judgment.

SPEAKING THE TRUTH IN LOVE

When we dads stop to think that parents average ten negative comments to their children for every positive comment, it is not hard to understand why kids so often seek refuge somewhere else. Most fathers, no matter how spiritual or conscientious, are more prone to send messages laced with criticism, commands, or demands.

That's why it's so important to watch our words. The apostle Paul admonishes us, "Do not let any unwholesome talk come out of your mouths, but only what is helpful for building others up according to their needs, that it may benefit those who listen" (Eph. 4:29).

What we say to them usually falls into one of two categories: (1) destructive, critical, unwholesome communication; or (2) positive, affirming, edifying communication.

Suppose you and I are in the same room. You recognize me and try to introduce yourself. You walk up to me, extend your hand, and start to say, "Hello, Josh, I'm . . ." But before you can even utter the next word, I reach out and slap you hard on the cheek! You're startled, hurt, and confused at my odd behavior. You stand off in the corner for a few minutes, pondering what to do. Finally, you decide to try again, a little more cautiously this time, watching for signals from me. Again my hand darts out to strike you. How many times will you continue to approach me?

Our words can be as vicious as a physical blow. Words hurt. Words leave wounds. If we lash out at our children with criticism, sarcasm, condemnation, and disgust, we will slam the door on their willingness to run to us when they're in trouble. But if on the other hand, we "speak the truth in love" (Eph. 4:15), handling even problem situations with a positive approach, we will promote ourselves to our children as places of refuge.

COMING ALONGSIDE OUR KIDS

The 1992 Olympics in Barcelona featured one of the most memorable moments in sports history. Derek Redmond of Great Britain was on his way to fulfilling a lifetime dream: winning a gold medal in the Olympics. He had earned a spot in the semifinals of the 400-meters, and as the gun sounded to begin the race, Derek got off to a great start. He was running the race of his life. The finish line was in sight, when suddenly he felt a stab of pain in his right leg. He pitched face-first to the track with a torn hamstring. The race was over for Derek.

He struggled to his feet before the medical team could reach him. Though every runner had passed him, he began hopping forward, tears of pain and disappointment streaking his face, determined to finish the race. Suddenly, a man plowed through the security guards on the sidelines and ran onto the track.

He raced up to Derek and hugged him. "You don't have to do this," Jim Redmond told his weeping son.

"Yes, I do," Derek answered.

"Well, then," his father said, "we're going to finish together."

Derek's father gripped his son around the shoulders and they faced the finish line, resolutely waving off the security men who hovered about them. They limped and hopped together, Derek's head sometimes buried in his father's shoulder, but they stayed in Derek's lane all the way to the end.

The watching crowd gaped at the unusual scene. Then one by one, they rose to their feet and began cheering and crying at the son's determination and the father's support.

How many times have I stayed in the stands when I should have run onto the track to support my kids? Too many, I must confess. But becoming a refuge to my children means running to their side, not to carry them but to come alongside them when they face hurt and disappointment. It means saying, "We're going to finish this together." It means enduring the stares of the crowd and ignoring the cries of the critics. It may be personally risky or professionally unwise, but it will be worth it to hear my kids say, "Thanks, Dad, you're my defender."

SETTING HEALTHY LIMITS

Becoming a refuge for our children doesn't require us to become overly permissive parents who never dare speak a word of correction or exercise discipline. Quite the contrary.

One day I was out for a walk on the mountainside near our home in Julian, California, when I came across a man who was traveling the United States in a covered wagon. He had stopped to graze his mules on a meadow nearby, and I struck up a conversation with him. It turned out that he was very experienced in raising animals, and I happened to ask, "What's the best environment for raising livestock here, like your mules? Open grazing land, a large fenced pasture, or a corral?"

Without hesitation, he answered, "Oh, the fenced pasture, by far."

"Why?" I asked.

"Because when animals get into that open grazing land, they get lost. Often they may be attacked by predators. Open grazing land is just too unsafe. And if you put them into a corral, they always have to be provided for. They can't roam around and provide for themselves. But when you put them into a good fenced pasture, all they need is right there and they can still operate on their own."

That conversation suggests a fantastic analogy from Scripture. Our loving Father has given us all we need in green pastures and still waters (Ps. 23:2). But he has also given us fences—his perfect law of liberty and the truth that sets us free in Christ (see James 1:25; John 8:32). Fenced pastures are not only good for livestock, they're good for children as well. Kids thrive within healthy limits when their parents are neither autocratic nor permissive.

A child will turn to a father as a refuge when that dad has established healthy limits that communicate concern and provide guidance for the child without exasperating him or her (see Eph. 6:4). Fathers are responsible for spelling out the boundaries for their children, boundaries that are built upon the loving foundation of a father's love, acceptance, and concern.

BUILDING A SUPPORT SYSTEM

American culture tends to portray men as independent, self-sufficient individuals who blaze their own trails. Many men have trouble admitting they have needs or problems. Many find it difficult to turn to others for help.

But becoming a refuge for our children requires the participation of a support system. In fact, it should involve the whole Christian community. There is great value in working together with others of like mind—your church, youth group, youth pastor, teachers, coaches, and family friends—to share resources, insights, and strengths, and to build safe places for our kids.

My wife, Dottie, and I were fortunate to find such a relationship with our friends Dick and Charlotte Day when our children were still small. We lived near each other. We spent lots of time together individually and as families. We vacationed together. We carpooled to school and church events. The Day family would take the McDowell kids with them on outings, and we would do the same with the Day kids.

That support network bore sweet fruit. One of Dick's sons once told him, "If you weren't my dad, I'd want Josh to be." And once, when I asked Heather who she thought was the greatest dad (other than me, of course!), she answered, "Dick." I was comforted by the knowledge that there was another "father figure" in my children's lives to whom they could turn in times of distress.

That kind of network has given my children a sense of security. I wanted them to turn to me for refuge, of course, but it helped both them *and* me to know they also had other adults to whom they could turn in a crisis.

If you do not have such a support system for you and your children, begin building one. Invite other Christians to work and pray together with you to that end. Quiz your kids about who they would feel comfortable talking to in a crisis. And don't be afraid to ask your friends how you could be more available and accessible to your kids and theirs.

Our kids are growing up in a stressful, demanding, often discouraging world. Some of them face incredible pressure at school, at home, even at church. They are often confused, disappointed, and insecure. But if they have a refuge—a safe place—then they can feel secure, believing that no matter what happens, their father will be there, believing in them, defending them, supporting them.

If our kids have that—if they know they can find refuge in their father—they will be less likely to seek refuge in drugs or alcohol. They will be less likely to seek refuge in the approval of their peers or in the company of questionable friends. They will be more likely to turn to Dad in a crisis, more likely to confide in their father, more likely to weather the storms that rage around them.

May each of our children find refuge in the Father.

And in us. In Dad.

For Reflection, Discussion, and Action

1. Is God truly a refuge for you? If so, why? What attributes or characteristics of your heavenly Father make you turn to him in times of trouble? How can you reflect those attributes or characteristics in your own life?

_____

_____

_____

_____

_____

_____

*2. Make a lunch or breakfast date for this coming week with each of your children (separately), and do what Norm Wakefield prescribed for the father who was having trouble communicating with his son. Make it your goal to spend the entire meal listening. Ask such questions as, "What are your biggest problems or concerns these days?" "Who do you most often talk to when you have a problem?" "Do you feel like you can come to me with your problems?" and "Are there any problems you think you'd have trouble talking to me about?"

*3. Identify one project or problem each of your kids needs help with right now. What can you do to come alongside that child and support him or her?

_____

_____

_____

_____

_____

_____

_____

4. What kind of support system (other than Mom and Dad) do your kids have? Are there adults in their lives they would feel confident and comfortable taking their troubles to? If you don't know, ask your kids. If the answer is no, consider how you might strengthen their support system.

*5. In the space provided below (or on a separate sheet of paper), make a list of the strategies you need to employ to become a refuge for your children. (Be as specific as possible.)

_____

_____

_____

_____

_____

_____

_____

_____

_____

_____

_____

_____

_____

_____

_____

_____

_____

_____

_____

_____

CHAPTER 9

The Father as Friend

Thirty-year-old Mike stood behind the pulpit at his father's funeral and choked back tears. Many had already paid tribute to a man who spent thirty-five-years in ministry before succumbing to cancer in his early fifties. The tributes extolled his love for God, his effectiveness with people and paperwork, his love for his family. Each of the speakers was sincere, offering loving memories of a life well lived. But Mike's tearful words paid tribute to his father in a way that no one else present could have done.

He told about sitting on his father's lap as a toddler, listening to story after story. Learning to ride a bike. Fishing trips. One-on-one basketball tournaments. Tennis matches. Body surfing at the beach together. His father's rare display of emotion when his only son graduated from high school, and again when he married, and again when he earned a college degree. And, of course, their long, intimate talks beside his dying father's hospital bedside.

"He was my best friend," Mike said, his voice choking with emotion. "I will miss my father. But I think I will miss my best friend more."

Contrast that tribute with the story told to me by the wife of a senior vice-president of a huge construction firm. She had heard me speak at a local church and later approached me in a restaurant. As she shook my hand, she started to cry.

"I have to share something with you," she said hesitantly. "My husband just died. He was a million-dollar-a-year man. He traveled all over the world building and constructing things, but he never took time for his children, even when he was home. All his children turned against him, and when they were grown, they would have nothing to do with him. On his deathbed, he confessed to me that he was dying one of the saddest men in the world. He told me, 'I gained prestige, but I lost my family.'"

I'm sure I don't have to tell you which of these two fathers I hope to emulate. I want to be the kind of father Mike had. I want to be the kind of father who enjoys his children's company, the kind of father whose daughter calls him at work "just to talk," the kind of father whose son asks him to be best man at his wedding. I want to be a father who is a friend to his children.

Such a task isn't easy for many men. Oh, it's probably better than it was a generation or two ago. Jerry Adler, writing in *Newsweek* magazine, relates:

> At the age of 49, Robert Blumenfeld, a San Francisco businessman, recalls exactly how many times his father played ball with him (once), and what his father said when he graduated from high school *cum laude*: that some other 18-year-old had just signed with a baseball team for $100,000. Dan Koenigshofer, a 46-year-old engineer in Chapel Hill, N.C., "can't ever recall that my dad said he loved me" (although he's sure that he *did* love him, in his taciturn 1950s way). David Weinstein, a Harvard economist, even knows where his father was when he was born, 32 years ago. He was in his office. Back then, the next day was soon enough for a new father to visit his son.[1]

We may not be quite like those fathers, but many of us still labor under a myriad of misconceptions about fatherhood. Some of us harbor the illusion that the ideal man is "macho," a tough, brawny individual who doesn't need anyone. Some of us have inherited the attitude that "men work and women take care of the kids." Some of us think that being a friend to our kids would be a sign of weakness. Some of us tend to think that our main job as fathers is to exercise power and authority over our wives and kids. Some of us are a bit nervous about intimacy in relationships, even afraid of it. Some of us honestly don't know how to be friends to our kids because we've never had that kind of relationship with our own fathers.

But regardless of how poor, distant, or faulty our relationships with our fathers were, we do have a model of the father as a friend. That model is found, of course, in our heavenly Father.

What a Friend We Have

Just as God's nature and character form the basis of all that we know to be right and good, so he is the standard for fatherhood. And the standard he models is of a Father who is also a friend to his children.

His availability and desire to be a friend to his children is exhibited throughout his interaction with men and women through the ages. Abraham, whose faith God rewarded by making him "the father of many nations" (Gen. 17:4–5; Rom. 4:17–18), is referred to throughout the Bible as the friend of God:

O our God, did you not drive out the inhabitants of this land before your people Israel and give it for ever to the descendants of Abraham your friend? (2 Chron. 20:7)

But you, O Israel, my servant, Jacob, whom I have chosen, you descendants of Abraham my friend . . . (Isa. 41:8)

And the scripture was fulfilled that says, "Abraham believed God, and it was credited to him as righteousness," and he was called God's friend. (James 2:23)

When the Israelites erected the tabernacle in the wilderness, and Moses would enter the tent to worship and confer with God, the pillar of cloud that signified God's presence would rest before the tabernacle entrance. At such times, the Bible says:

> The LORD would speak to Moses face to face, as a man speaks with his friend. (Exod. 33:11)

When God spoke through the prophet Samuel and told Saul, the first king of Israel, that he had forfeited his crown and his kingdom, Samuel also announced the coming reign of David, whose friendship with God is referred to in memorable terms:

> But now your kingdom will not endure; the LORD has sought out a man after his own heart and appointed him leader of his people, because you have not kept the LORD's command. (1 Sam. 13:14)

The phrase by which Samuel referred to David—"a man after his own heart"—indicated a rare kinship, a rare friendship, a rare intimacy.

Like Abraham, Moses, and David, we have the privilege of calling our Father our friend. Our heavenly Father is a friend to his children. He is available to us. He longs to spend time with us, revealing himself to us. He knows us and is always seeking for us to know him better. He enjoys our company. He revels in our laughter, glories in our praise, and delights in our victories.

It's important to note that God does not have to choose between being our Father and our friend. He does not neglect one in favor of the other. He is our Father; that is his nature. He is our friend; that is a reflection of his nature. Being a friend to a child is part of what being a father is all about.

That's the kind of father I want to be—both a father and a friend to my children. I want my friendship with my children to be a natural reflection of my fatherhood, and I will not sacrifice my responsibility as father in a misguided effort to earn my kids' friendships. But one thing I learn from my Father is that it is not necessary to do so. What *is* necessary, if I am ever to resemble my heavenly Father, is for me to rely on him day by day through his Holy Spirit, seeking his help in implementing the strategies that will foster true friendship with my kids.

BEING AVAILABLE

Suppose you're a good friend of the boss at a large company. It's Friday, and you need to see your friend on short notice, so you go over to his office and ask his secretary if you could possibly talk to him for just a few minutes.

"I'm sorry," the secretary tells you, "but he's booked solid until next Tuesday. You'll have to come back then."

"Look," you say, an apologetic smile on your face, "I won't take much of his time. Please just tell him I really need to see him. It'll only take a minute."

The secretary calls the boss and tells him you're here. She mentions your name, but you hear the boss's voice on the intercom, saying, "I can't be disturbed. Schedule a meeting for next Tuesday."

How would that exchange make you feel? How do you think the boss's response would reflect on your friendship? Would you still consider that person a close friend? You would probably tend to think that your estimation of that friendship was different from the boss's.

That's how our kids feel when we aren't available to them. Oh, I know there are times when you can't stop what you're doing right that minute. You can't always drop everything to answer a toddler's question or play catch with your little leaguer. But most of us can be a lot more available than we are.

I was at a crucial point in finishing a manuscript to meet a deadline when Sean, who was seven years old at the time, approached me. I cut him off without even letting him speak.

"Not now, Sean," I said, "I've got to finish this manuscript."

My disappointed son had no sooner left the study than Dottie entered the room.

"Honey," she said, "you're always going to have deadlines. But you're not always going to have a seven-year-old son wanting his daddy's time."

She was right, and I knew it. Without a moment's hesitation, I put down my pen, pushed the large, comfortable chair away from the desk, and hurried to find Sean.

That was one of many lessons I had in availability. I learned that my friendship with my kids required not only attention—taking them out for breakfast, going to Disneyland together—but also availability—being there when they were ready to talk, listen, or just to share a few quiet moments in each other's presence.

BEING TRANSPARENT

Children face many struggles as they grow up. If the adults they follow appear perfect and infallible—like gods—children may see themselves as inferior, and may perceive their struggles as evidence that something is wrong with them. Living among "gods" can be very intimidating. Our children need relationships with adults who are capable of appropriate transparency.

Transparency can be either appropriate or inappropriate. *Inappropriate transparency* involves self-disclosures that are detrimental to children. The father who constantly berates himself, condemns his own actions as stupid, or repeatedly recounts all his failures is practicing inappropriate transparency. He models low self-esteem, which in turn fosters insecurity in his children. The children see their father as incompetent and will be unlikely to turn to him in time of need.

Appropriate transparency allows the children to see inside their dad. They hear their father talk about his own experiences as a child and youth. They discover how Dad perceives himself, his masculinity, his role in life. Appropriate transparency helps children gain insight into how their father handles failure, success, disappointment, praise, and criticism. Appropriate transparency also includes the ability to express feelings. Many men learn to suppress their feelings instead of expressing them. Tears are taboo for such men. But if you feel free to talk and laugh and cry about your joys, disappointments, fears, and longings, you will help your children get to know you. And in so doing, you will open the door to friendship.

ASKING OPEN-ENDED QUESTIONS

Something I worked at very hard was asking my children questions that could get a conversation going, questions that helped us get to know each other better (and thus, of course, deepen our friendships). I'd do this while driving a car, walking, or standing in line with them at the bank. Some of the questions I've asked include:

"If you could change our family, how would you change it?" (Brace yourself for that answer!)

"If you were the father of this family, what would you do differently?" (Brace yourself for the answer to this one, too!)

"When did you have the most fun?"

"When was the last time you felt embarrassed?"

"When did you cry the hardest?"

"When have you felt closest to God?"

"If you had a million dollars, what would you do with it?"

"If you could ask God one question, what would it be?"

"If you could visit any place in the world, where would you like to go?"

Once after we'd been to the zoo, we had a fairly long ride home. As we left the parking lot, I said, "Kids, let's play a little game. What animal did you see today that best describes you— and why?"

For the next sixty miles, Dottie and I got tremendous insights into what our kids thought about themselves. Little Katie—she was about three-and-a-half at the time—said she believed she was like the bears.

"Why?" I asked.

"Because I like to be hugged," she said.

Katie was sitting in the back seat, so I pulled the car over to the side of the road, got out, went around to her side of the car and opened her door so I could give her a "bear hug" before we continued our trip.

CULTIVATING MUTUAL INTERESTS

"I offered to take my kid out to have a good time," a father once told me, "but he didn't have any fun at all. The whole thing was a big failure."

"What did you do with him?" I asked.

"Well," the man explained, "I love golf, so I took him golfing." Then he frowned. "It turns out he hates golfing, so I guess that's that."

Okay, this father wanted to spend time with his son, but only on *his terms*, at *his convenience*. He would have been much more successful if he had cultivated mutual interests with his son.

Mutual interests foster friendship. Look at your own circle of friendships. You may have "golf buddies" or "fishing buddies." You've got "college chums," "frat brothers," or "Army buddies." You've gone to auctions or antique car shows with friends. Your friends are your friends partly because they go to church with you or they go to sporting events with you. That's because mutual interests foster friendship.

The wise father begins to build mutual interests with his children when they are young. The man who reads to his preschooler builds a point of contact to share books and ideas in later life. It thrills me whenever my children come to me now and say, "Dad, you've got to read this book; I think you'll really like it."

It's never too late, however, to develop mutual interests with your kids. When my son Sean was around ten, he developed an interest in sports cars (and I mean the expensive ones—the Maseratis, the Lamborghinis, the Ferrari Testarossas). As I saw Sean finding pictures of these cars in magazines and newspaper ads, I could see his interest was more than casual.

So I got an idea. I grabbed the Yellow Pages and picked out some of the top sports car dealers in Beverly Hills. Then I sent each car dealer a letter that said:

> I'm a desperate dad. I'll do anything to spend time with my son, and right now he's into sports cars. Would it be possible, if I pulled him out of school and brought him to your showroom, for him to take some test drives?

I told each dealer up front that I was not interested in buying a car, yet to my amazement, not one dealer turned me down. I called and made appointments, and Sean and I drove the 150 miles to Beverly Hills for a day in the sports car showrooms. And what a day it was! Sean went out alone on test drives with salesmen, trying out just about every big name car you can think of. As they rolled by the showroom each time, a proud Sean would wave to me through the car window.

The drive home that afternoon gave me a great opportunity to talk with my son about riches and possessions and materialism. But more importantly, it drew us closer together and added a little more depth and breadth to our friendship.

MAKING AN EXTRA EFFORT

A reporter once came to our home to interview me for a magazine article. Even though she was writing for a Christian publication, it became apparent that she was trying to find something negative about me that might help sell copies. She turned to my son Sean, then eight, who was watching us. "What is the one thing you don't like about your dad?" she asked my young son.

"Nothing," Sean replied.

She kept prodding him, with no results. Then she smiled and coaxed, "You've got to have *one* thing you don't like about your dad!"

Finally, Sean came up with something. "I don't like when he goes away."

The reporter's face lit up, and her expression indicated she had found a scoop that would spice up her article.

After the interview, as my guest was leaving, I mentioned that she owed it to journalistic integrity to also ask Sean what he *liked* most about his dad. After some persuasion, she did. Sean immediately responded, "He spends a lot of time with me."

The reporter seemed puzzled by the apparent inconsistency. I explained to her that my son's answers were consistent with what I have always desired from my children: (1) that they will never like their dad being away from them, and (2) that they will always feel their dad spends a lot of time with them.

Like many men whose responsibilities take them away from home, I often found it difficult to juggle a heavy travel schedule and my family responsibilities. I wasn't always successful, but I made an extra effort to build friendships with my kids. I took my children with me on trips whenever possible, one at a time, arranging my responsibilities on the road ahead of time to insure a lot of personal time with each child. I also tried to call home every day and talk to most of the family.

Once, when I had to miss one of Sean's high school basketball games because of a trip to Russia, I made arrangements to call him at halftime on a cell phone my wife took to the game (back when cell phones were a real novelty). It wasn't as good as being there—and it made me miss him even more—but it communicated to him (and his teammates, as it turned out) how important he was to me.

When I returned from trips, I scheduled extra time for each of my kids (take each one out to breakfast, pick them up after school) and made the most of every moment we had together.

GETTING TO KNOW THEIR FRIENDS

Another strategy for being both father and friend is to get to know your kids' friends. Dottie and I loved to host our kids and their friends in our home. (Dottie was the original "Kool Aid Mom!") We tried to include our kids' friends regularly on our spe-

cial outings and family events. And I often agreed to play chauf-
feur because I discovered I could learn a lot from what I could see
in the rearview mirror.

For example, I once took Kelly and her friends to a Lakers
game, and managed to glance occasionally at the road in between a fascinating study of teenage girls and their friendships. I
watched Kelly and her friends in the rearview mirror, alert to what
they talked about, what things seemed to interest them, and how
Kelly fit in. I wanted to know: Is she ever arrogant? Is she timid
among friends? Does she make an effort to include everyone? Is
she generous? The basketball game provided more opportunities
to witness how Kelly interacted with her friends, and a stop at a
restaurant for ice cream sundaes on the way home gave me even
more insight. All in all, it was a full evening, one that provided
hours of enjoyment and an education for a father interested in
being a friend to his daughter.

DEVELOPING TRADITIONS

When my children were younger, we had a tradition that
many of our friends and house guests thought was odd. No matter
who was visiting or what was going on, I would excuse myself and
go to bed with the children.

If we were having guests over, they were told ahead of time,
"At 6:30 or 7:00, Josh will be unavailable." We also told people,
"Don't phone Josh between 6:30 and 9:00 p.m. because he'll be
with the children."

Those two-and-a-half hours belonged to me and my children.
Sometimes we went for a walk. Sometimes we wrestled on the
floor. Sometimes we read a book together.

One of our favorite activities was getting in the jacuzzi that
had been installed in our bedroom as a gift from friends. Sometimes we just talked. Sometimes we watched game shows on TV
while relaxing in the jacuzzi. One night, just for fun, we filled a
huge Tupperware® bowl with popcorn and floated it in the water.
It swirled around and around and everybody had ample oppor-

tunity to dip in. The kids talked about that one for weeks, and I even heard back from teachers and other dads about the "popcorn in the jacuzzi."

Such traditions can be like sunlight and water to your friend-ships with your kids, helping them take root and grow. One family of my acquaintance practices a "progressive supper" of sorts with their family in a nearby mall. They make the rounds of all the restaurants in the mall's food court, ordering the least expensive item on each menu and sharing it among the four of them.

Whatever traditions you develop, make sure they're fun for everyone, and that they give ample opportunity for conversation and interaction with each other. (Watching a movie, for example, is not the best tradition because there's little chance for interac-tion. A game of miniature golf, on the other hand, can supply a couple hours of conversation.)

A father who is available and transparent with his kids, who asks probing questions and cultivates mutual interests with his kids, who gets to know his kids' friends, makes an extra effort in his relationship with his kids, and builds meaningful traditions in his family will go a long way toward being the kind of father the Father is . . . both a father and a friend.

Such a father provides more than friendship for his kids. He provides his kids an education in relationships, a model of what healthy friendship looks like. He provides a firewall of protection against dangerous and damaging friendships. He provides prepa-ration for his kids to interact socially with their peers throughout adolescence and into adulthood. He provides a friendship that, in the midst of the many changes and challenges of adolescence, will always be there. And he provides an incentive for his children to develop a friendship with God, their Father in heaven.

For Reflection, Discussion, and Action

*Read through the following situations. Ask yourself, "Is this typical of me?" Use your answers to help evaluate your relationship with your child.

Yes No

❏ ❏ 1. Immediately after dinner, you leave the table to watch television or read the newspaper.

❏ ❏ 2. You occasionally talk to your children about your own childhood, sharing your own insecurities as a boy and how you coped with them.

❏ ❏ 3. You've never cried in front of your children.

❏ ❏ 4. You regularly stop what you're doing to help your children with schoolwork.

❏ ❏ 5. At the supper table, one of your children starts to tell about an incident that happened in class; you change the subject.

❏ ❏ 6. You look forward to spending time with your children.

❏ ❏ 7. You can't name any interests you have in common with your children.

❏ ❏ 8. You have at least one special pursuit that you share with each of your kids.

❏ ❏ 9. Your children know nothing about your most recent worries, failures, or disappointments.

❏ ❏ 10. You can name the three best friends of each of your kids.

Answering "yes" to any of the odd-numbered questions indicate areas in which improvement is needed. Answering "yes" to the even-numbered questions indicates areas in which you're apparently doing well.

CHAPTER 10
The Father Who Disciplines

One morning, I came into the kitchen and saw that my son Sean had forgotten to take out the garbage, a chore which was clearly defined as having to be done before he left for school each day. Sean had already left for school.

"I've got to go get him and bring him back so he can take out the garbage," I told Dottie.

"Josh," she answered, "you can't. It's time for school to start in just a few minutes. He'll be penalized for being late."

"Honey, I've got to do it," I insisted. So I got in my car, drove to the school, and found Sean on the playground shooting some baskets before the first bell had rung.

I went up to Sean. "Son," I said, "I want you to get your bike and head back up to the house and do the garbage."

"But Dad," Sean protested, "it's five minutes to the bell. Can't I do it after school?"

"No, son, you were supposed to do it before you left for school, and I'd like you to do it right now, please."

"Dad, couldn't you do it for me—just once?"

"No, son," I answered, "it's your responsibility."

Sean flipped the ball back to his buddies and trudged to his bike, shoulders slumped. As I watched him ride away, I heard a little voice in my ear. "What kind of dad are you, McDowell? It wouldn't hurt to take out the garbage for your son just once, would it?"

By the time Sean performed his simple chore and rode his bike back to school, the bell had rung, and he was a good thirty minutes late for class. Sean's teacher sent him to the principal's office as soon as he arrived, and he had to explain to the principal exactly what I had done. The principal wrote Sean an excuse and sent him back to class. Then he called me.

"I can't believe what Sean just told me," he said. "I gave him an excuse back to class because I was so impressed that a parent would hold his kid responsible. If more parents taught responsibility to their children, our job would be much easier." Hanging up the phone, I felt a tremendous surge of relief. I had felt like an ogre for being so picky with Sean about a bag of garbage, but the principal's words assured me that I had acted wisely.

None of us wants to be an ogre as a father. Likewise, none of us wants to be a pushover. I didn't want to be unreasonable with Sean, but I did want to provide correction to a problem. I wanted to help him accept responsibility. I wanted to help him develop self-discipline. I wanted to offer appropriate guidance to him. I wanted to be the kind of father my Father is.

The Father's Discipline

God is good. He is a loving Father—a perfect Father. His intentions and actions are never evil or unloving. Yet he disciplines his children, not *in spite* of his goodness but *because* of his goodness, not *in spite* of his love but *because* of his love. He doesn't discipline us because *he* is imperfect but because *we* are.

The Scriptures repeatedly reveal our heavenly Father as a Father who disciplines:

Know then in your heart that as a man disciplines his son,
so the LORD your God disciplines you. (Deut. 8:5)

The LORD disciplines those he loves, as a father the son he delights in. (Prov. 3:12)

The man who offers wise correction and appropriate discipline to his son or daughter is reflecting the nature and character of God. It is for that reason that God's Word extols the wisdom of fathers who discipline their children (Prov. 23:13; 29:17) and describes tragedy in the lives of those who do not (1 Sam. 2:22–4:18; 1 Kings 1:1–53). The writer of Hebrews provides a fairly extensive view of godly discipline:

> Do not make light of the Lord's discipline, and do not lose heart when he rebukes you, because the Lord disciplines those he loves, and he punishes everyone he accepts as a son. Endure hardship as discipline; God is treating you as sons. For what son is not disciplined by his father? If you are not disciplined (and everyone undergoes discipline), then you are illegitimate children and not true sons. Moreover, we have all had human fathers who disciplined us and we respected them for it. How much more should we submit to the Father of our spirits and live! Our fathers disciplined us for a little while as they thought best; but God disciplines us for our good, that we may share in his holiness. No discipline seems pleasant at the time, but painful. Later on, however, it produces a harvest of righteousness and peace for those who have been trained by it. (Heb. 12:5–11)

Yes, godly discipline produces respect, peace, and a harvest of righteousness! That's what we want for our children! That's what we hope and pray to produce in them, with God's help, by reflecting our Father's nature and character, by becoming a father who disciplines.

No, we don't want to discipline our children out of anger or arrogance; we want to discipline them as God disciplines us—out of love (Heb. 12:6). We don't want to discipline our children to make *our* lives easier; we want to discipline them as God disciplines us—for their good (Heb. 12:10). We don't want to discipline our children to feed our egos or meet our needs; we want to discipline them as God disciplines us—to produce a harvest of righteousness and peace in them (Heb. 12:11).

We want to be the kind of father our Father is.

Four Parenting Styles

There are basically four parenting styles that can be found among parents:

- Autocratic—"You'll do it my way or else!"
- Permissive—"You can do anything you want."
- Neglectful—"I don't really care what you do."
- Relational—"I'm listening . . . I care about you . . . I want to understand . . . This time we'll do it this way because. . . "

Each style reveals a certain attitude toward the use of authority by the parent. The autocratic father is an "absolute ruler," whom Webster defines at three levels. First, there is the dictator who "holds and exercises absolute power." At a slightly less ominous level, the autocrat is one who is "invested with or assumes absolute independent power over others." At the very least, an autocrat is any "domineering, self-willed person."

When autocratic parents wield absolute power over children, they impose many limits but communicate little love. Many autocrats give children "good homes." They feed and clothe their kids and seem to provide everything needed for a normal life—except, in most cases, enough support and love.

Living in an autocracy causes children to react in one of two ways: fight or flight. When children choose *flight*, they typically withdraw and learn to go along and "be obedient"—at least on the surface. Inside, however, they are seething. When children choose to *fight*, their anger is out in the open. They complain, talk back, and even lash out verbally or physically, because a father who tries to lay down rules apart from a real relationship with his kids is sowing the seeds of rebellion.

One study of adolescent/parent relationships revealed that children reared by autocratic parents are likely to exhibit hostility toward their parents, prejudice toward older people, anti-social tendencies (and the accompanying actions, such as stealing, lying, fighting, and vandalism), feelings of social alienation, rejection of traditional moral standards, and an inability to relate well to other people.

The other extreme, of course, is permissiveness. Some fathers are strong on support but wimpy on discipline. Permissively parented kids often hold their parents hostage. Younger children may refuse to take naps, refuse to eat at mealtimes, and resort to temper tantrums or screaming fits when they don't get their way. Older kids may speak disrespectfully to Mom and Dad, come and go as they please at all hours of the day or night, and expect their parents to provide whatever they want when they want it. Permissively parented children get their way a lot, but they are no happier than children in autocratic homes because a healthy balance of love and limits is not there. They seldom want to live according to their parents' moral standards, and are likely to become involved in drinking, drug abuse, and other self-indulgent behavior. They are more susceptible to sexual immorality and pathology.

In order to have the proper balance of love and limits, fathers need to take a relational approach, in which both love and limits are clearly communicated to the kids. The children feel loved, which adds to their sense of worth, but they are also aware of their limits, which adds to their sense of security. Kids respond to rules, but only in the context of relationship.

Once again, this is the model our heavenly Father shows us. He laid down rules for his children. After all, he gave the Ten Commandments, right? But he only gave his people the Ten Commandments after generations of relationship with them. He started with just one rule—"You must not eat from the tree of the knowledge of good and evil" (Gen. 2:17)—and then spent many years revealing himself and developing a relationship with his children before laying down the Law on Mt. Sinai.

That's the kind of father we all want to be, even though we know we can't do it. We've tried and failed many times before. But our model Father can do it. He's done it for eons, and he can do it in us and through us if we rely on him through his Holy Spirit and keep in mind a few helpful tactics:

DISCIPLINING IN THE CONTEXT OF A RELATIONSHIP

Discipline is always most effective in the context of a thriving, loving relationship. So when correcting your children, begin by asking a question that appeals to your relationship with them. If the answer to that question is positive, then you can be confident that they will respond to your correction. Ask, for example, "Do you know that I love you?" By asking that question before you offer correction, you appeal to them not on the basis of your authority but on the basis of our relationship.

I once spoke in the Philippines to over six hundred pastors and Christian workers. Afterward, over two hundred of those men lined up to talk to me. One of the major problems I dealt with that night was illustrated by one of them—a father and pastor—who told me his family had turned against him. His three children—seventeen, thirteen, and ten years of age—were considered to be "the worst kids in the church" and were all rebelling in one way or another. He wanted to know what he could do.

"Forget the rules," I told him.

"What?" he said in disbelief. "That's what's wrong. They're not obeying any rules. They don't even think they need to."

"I know what you're saying," I told him, "but I repeat, forget emphasizing the rules. Start building a relationship. You don't have anything to lose."[1]

No matter how old your children are, it's not too late to begin building relationships. I recall a Portland woman whose four adult children had completely rebelled against her and caused her untold agony and heartache. Dick Day and I shared the relationship-building principles from *How to Be a Hero to Your Kids*, and she went home committed to the long, hard task of rebuilding those relationships. Five years later, we met that woman again. She said that her relationship with two of her children had turned around 180 degrees! She shared tearfully how attention to relationship, even with adult children, had paid rich dividends.

COMMUNICATING RULES CLEARLY

Family psychologist John Rosemond says that effective parents "communicate their rules clearly. They don't 'beat around the bush' when it comes to what they expect. They don't plead, bribe, or threaten. They simply and straightforwardly tell their children what they can do, can't do, and must do."[2] Yes, fenced pastures make healthy sheep. And clear, reasonable limits make healthy, happy kids.

Volumes have been written on how to be an effective parent. One expert emphasizes one thing; a second expert contradicts the first. But I have found no better advice than a verse from one of Paul's letters, which says, "Fathers, do not provoke your children to anger; bring them up in the discipline and instruction of the Lord" (Eph. 6:4, NASB). One of the surest ways for a father to provoke his children is to issue indistinct, unclear rules and standards to his children.

Some fathers might tell a daughter, for example, "I expect you home at a decent hour, young lady." But what's a decent hour? That's open to interpretation. One o'clock in the morning may seem like a decent hour to a seventeen-year-old, while her father may have been pacing the floor since eleven o'clock. It is much better to communicate the limit clearly, to say instead, "Please be home by 11:00—not 11:30 or even 11:10."

Instead of telling a young teen, "Your chore is to take out the trash," both father and teen will be much better off if it's clear that "your chore is to take out the trash every morning before you leave for school." Instead of "Go clean your room," tell them, "I'd like you to clean your room by dinner time, and that includes dusting and running the sweeper."

Clearly communicating rules and expectations helps a father establish boundaries, helps a child honor boundaries, and helps both avoid confusion and misunderstanding.

MAKING THE PAYOFF FOR MISBEHAVIOR SMALL

It helps to remember that when children do something wrong, they're usually seeking attention. Now, obviously, you can't ignore your child when he or she misbehaves. You have to deal with it. But the question is, *how* do you deal with it? What does the child see and hear as you respond to misbehavior?

If a child can get you to raise your voice, if he can get you red in the face, if he can provoke you in any number of ways, he is likely to conclude that misbehavior is the best way to get your attention. On the other hand, if you can deal with his misbehavior quietly, without long lectures or other angry outbursts, the payoff will not be nearly as big.

One simple approach is to quietly tell the child that this kind of thing won't be tolerated and, if necessary, to separate him from the rest of the family for a while. Remember, it's harder to get attention when you're all alone. The "chair in the corner" may seem like an old-fashioned idea, but with many children it is still extremely effective.

I realize it isn't always that simple, but however you deal with a child's misbehavior, keep in mind that kids are bound to do *some* things wrong. They are bound to misbehave on occasion simply because they are children. Make it your goal not to make such a big issue out of their negative behavior. Instead, try to accentuate their *positive* behavior.

As I mentioned earlier, try to catch them doing something right, and reinforce that behavior.

PLANNING AHEAD

Many fathers make their jobs more difficult by failing to plan ahead in matters of discipline. Effective parents, says family psychologist John Rosemond, "don't wait for problems to develop before doing something about them."[3]

For example, when your daughter returns home an hour after curfew, you're likely to seethe and simmer until she comes in the door, unless you've planned ahead and considered how you would react if she missed curfew. Or if your four-year-old often throws tantrums in the grocery store, do you wait until it happens again until you deal with it, or do you plan a reasonable, constructive response ahead of time so that you're not thrown off balance the next time it happens?

A pastor friend of mine tells how, when his son was seventeen, he and his wife began to worry that the young man was sexually involved with his girlfriend. They tried repeatedly—and sensitively, they thought—to express their acceptance and love for their son, encouraging him to confide in them. But he insisted that they had not become sexually active. The father and mother didn't totally drop the matter, but discussed between themselves how they would respond if the son did confess to being sexually involved or if the girlfriend became pregnant.

Within a few weeks, the son and his girlfriend sat in the pastor's home and tearfully broke the news. The girlfriend was indeed pregnant.

"It was a difficult moment, of course," the father says now, "but I am so glad my wife and I talked about how we would react ahead of time. I don't know what I'd have done if we hadn't. I might have gotten angry or said something I would have regretted later. But because we had already discussed how we would react to that situation, we were able to respond in a really healthy way."

Not every situation is that difficult, of course, but planning your response before it's necessary to respond can help in both simple and severe situations.

EMPLOYING NATURAL CONSEQUENCES

I believe that Scripture teaches two modes of positive discipline. One is disciplining by *natural consequences*.

Jesus' parable of the prodigal son is an excellent illustration of the corrective power of natural consequences. The young man in the story decided to leave home and live it up, and he demanded that his father give him his share of his inheritance. The father knew what would happen but handed the money over anyway. He apparently decided to let the boy learn a few lessons the hard way: by suffering the natural consequences of his actions.

Natural consequences took their toll. The boy spent all his money, lost his job, lost his friends, and wound up eating with the pigs. Only then, Jesus said, did he come "to his senses" (Luke 15:17). It took natural consequences to make the son see his need to return home to his father, where he was accepted and loved more than ever (Luke 15:11–32).

It is interesting that the father not only let him go but gave him his inheritance. Many fathers may let their son go, but how many would give him an inheritance to throw away? The father of the prodigal, however, may have valued the opportunity for his son to learn a huge lesson more than the money.

In our book, *How to Be a Hero to Your Kids*, Dick Day told of using natural consequences to teach his son Jonathan an important lesson when the boy was very small:

> We had an open fireplace in our home that was at floor level, and I often worried about Jonathan when he was around it. Not realizing what fire could do, he could reach into the fireplace and get terribly burned while Charlotte and I weren't looking.
>
> One evening we were sitting at dinner eating by candlelight. Jonathan started to reach up to touch the candle flame, and Charlotte started to stop him, but I said, "No, let him do it."

Jonathan stuck his finger in the flame and withdrew it immediately with a cry of pain. He wasn't burned badly, but he was burned just enough to learn the power of fire and to respect it. Some people might say it was cruel to let Jonathan stick his finger into the candle flame, but I don't think so. I'd much rather have him learn that fire burns from a tiny flame than from a roaring blaze.[4]

The father who lets his fifth-grader be brought home in a police car for shoplifting from the convenience store is employing the corrective power of natural consequences. The father who tearfully watches his daughter lose her position on the volleyball team because of low grades is employing the corrective power of natural consequences. The sorrowing father who lets his son spend a night in jail for "driving under the influence" is employing the corrective power of natural consequences.

SPECIFYING LOGICAL CONSEQUENCES

The other mode of discipline described in Scripture is *logical consequences*. This simply means that the parent determines with the child that certain consequences will happen if the child doesn't fulfill his responsibilities or misbehaves in a certain way. For example, "If you don't eat all your dinner, you get no dessert," or "If you don't feed your puppy, *you* don't eat, either."

We see the precedent for logical consequences taking place in the Garden of Eden. God laid everything out for them and, as I mentioned earlier, stipulated that the one tree they could not eat from was the tree of the knowledge of good and evil. If they did eat from that tree, God said, they would suffer the logical consequences—they would "surely die" (Gen. 2:15–17).

Of course, Eve did eat the fruit. Then Adam followed suit, and the consequences followed swiftly. Adam and Eve became subject to physical death and all its related penalties, such as pain in childbirth, painful toil, and banishment from Paradise itself (see Gen. 3:1–19).

God had spelled out the boundaries in which Adam and Eve could operate, and when they chose to violate those limits, they chose the consequences. God still loved them, but he enforced the logical consequences they had chosen.

Once again, an illustration from Dick Day's parenting experience aptly illustrates the corrective power of logical consequences:

> When my oldest son, Dick, got his driver's license, he and I agreed that if he got any moving violations, he would pay the fine and lose his driving privileges for thirty days. I can still remember the day Dick got his first moving violation. He came in timidly and said, "Dad, I got a ticket." I don't know what Dick expected, but all I said was, "Where are the car keys?"
>
> Dick handed me the keys. He also paid the fine, and he didn't drive the car for thirty days. There was no lecture. There was no asking him to explain "Why did you do that?" The logical consequences had already been spelled out, and Dick knew he was paying a price he had already agreed upon.[5]

Using the corrective power of logical consequences eliminates the need for lengthy lectures, explanations, arguments, and shouting matches. When both father and child know that certain actions carry certain logical, reasonable consequences, the matter is decided as soon as the action is taken.

The power of logical consequences can be extremely liberating for both father and child. The father doesn't have to be cast in the role of policeman, judge, or executioner. He simply enforces the consequences the young person—by his or her behavior—has chosen.

STICKING TO YOUR GUNS

My oldest daughter, Kelly, once called home from an eighth-grade graduation party at another student's home. She asked if she could stay overnight. I listened to her request and then asked a few questions. Kelly admitted that there would be boys at the "extended" party and, no, she couldn't be positive there would be no drinking. When she told me the names of some of those who were planning to stay past ten o'clock, I recognized the name of one boy who had a reputation for being able to obtain alcohol even though, like Kelly, he was only fourteen.

After hearing Kelly out, I replied, "No, Kelly, I don't think so. I want you to come home when the party ends at ten o'clock."

Kelly called back three times in the next half hour. At one point she began to cry into the phone, and then I learned what was really happening. Four or five of the other girls also wanted to stay overnight, but they had to get their parents' permission, too—and everything depended on what Kelly McDowell's dad said.

It was obvious that Kelly was being pressured by her peer group. She began telling me there probably wasn't much to worry about. Parents would be in the house and there would be lots of kids around. Nobody would be alone with anybody else.

I could tell that Kelly was feeding me lines her friends were giving her, and I stuck with my original ruling.

"Sorry, Kelly," I said, "but you'll have to come home."

I hung up with my daughter's sniffles ringing in my ears. I didn't like disappointing her, but I knew I had done the right thing. Later, when Kelly got home, she woke Dottie and me up and thanked us for telling her she couldn't stay overnight!

"Daddy," she said, "I didn't really want to stay, especially after you said no and the other girls started to pressure me. Thanks for helping me out."

I have discovered that when parents make a stand and stick to their guns, it does two things for their kids. First, it helps them deal with the peer group because they can say, "My parents won't let me." Second, and even more important, it lets the child know there are values and standards that can't be ignored or compromised.

ACTING IN LOVE, NOT ANGER

"The Lord disciplines those he loves," Proverbs 3:12 says. Notice that the Bible doesn't say, "The Lord disciplines those he hates." It doesn't even say, "The Lord disciplines those he's angry with." He disciplines in love, not in anger.

Every father gets angry with his children. But a wise father will be careful when administering discipline at such times. If you are red-faced or shouting, you're in no condition to offer loving correction to your child. If you feel like lashing out at someone verbally or inflicting hurt on someone, you're in no condition to offer loving correction to your child.

That's why it's so valuable, as I said earlier, to couch your correction in terms of your relationship with your children, to ask a child *before* you offer discipline, "Do you know that I love you?" This simple exercise not only places your correction in the context of your relationship, but it accomplishes something else—something just as valuable (perhaps even more so, at times). It serves as a correction to *you*, reminding you that if you want to be a father in the image of your heavenly Father, you need to discipline your children in love, not anger.

ADJUSTING YOUR PLAN

Some parents are rigidly consistent. They treat a child fundamentally the same when he's sixteen as when he was six. Their approach is to control the child from the cradle to the grave . . . or at least until he leaves home. This approach, however, can leave a child feeling smothered, hemmed in, stifled, often causing him to react in unwise and unhealthy ways. He has not only never learned self-control; he has come to despise any control.

But that's not the way our Father deals with us. The writer of Hebrews said that "God disciplines us for our good, that we may share in his holiness" (Heb. 12:10). In other words, he disciplines us so that we may grow up, become holy, become mature—that we may become more like him.

The wise father will reflect the Father's image in this way as well, adjusting his discipline to the child's age and maturity. He will discern when the child is ready for a new challenge, responsibility, or privilege, and will loosen the *external* discipline on the child to permit the development of *internal* discipline.

A father may say to squabbling siblings, for example, "This is not something I need to get involved in. I think you're both old enough to work this disagreement out between yourselves." A father of a teen may say, "I think you're old enough to set your alarm and get yourself out of bed in the morning," or "As long as you're making the grades in school, you can go to bed when you like."

The point is, effective discipline requires both consistency and flexibility—consistency in the application and enforcement of discipline, and flexibility in adjusting rules and expectations as kids grow and mature.

The child whose father provides godly discipline—discipline that is loving, clear, and consistent—is likely to reap a harvest of respect, peace, and righteousness. He equips his children to learn self-discipline, a quality that will help them lead lives that are emotionally, socially, spiritually, and physically healthy. He helps his children avoid the often tragic consequences of unwise behavior. He enables his children to enjoy the blessing of a good reputation. He promotes harmony in his children's minds and hearts, and in their relationships with others.

That's what God's discipline accomplishes in me, and that's what I wish for my children.

For Reflection, Discussion, and Action

*1. According to this chapter, there are four basic parenting styles: autocratic, permissive, neglectful, and relational. Which styles operated in your home as you were growing up? Which style most characterizes your approach to discipline?

_____
_____
_____

*2. Hebrews 12:10 mentions the object of God's discipline of his children ("that we may share in his holiness"). On the lines below, define what you consider to be your objects in disciplining your children:

I discipline my children that _____

_____

I discipline my children that _____

_____

I discipline my children that _____

_____

3. Do you ever use natural or logical consequences in disciplining your children? Think of some examples. If you'd like to start using logical consequences, start slowly in little ways and always stick to your guns when the logical consequences must be enforced.

_____
_____
_____
_____

4. Examine your attitude as you discipline your children. Put an "x" on the following lines to indicate the degree to which you are:

Critical	Correcting
Judgmental	Teaching
Manipulative	Guiding
Controlling	Releasing

What steps do you need to take to become more like the Father in the above ways?

_____

_____

_____

_____

_____

_____

*5. Do you more often discipline out of love, or out of anger? What concrete steps can you take to improve in this area?

_____

_____

_____

_____

_____

_____

_____

_____

_____

_____

_____

_____

CHAPTER 11
The Father and Forgiveness

I heard Don's story from a mutual friend. Don is the father of three daughters and a son. He has raised his family in the church, and he and his wife have faithfully and sensitively raised each child according to biblical principles. But when his youngest daughter reached her late teens, she became sexually active.

Actually, to be blunt, she became sexually promiscuous. Don and his wife tried everything they could think of to help her, but nothing seemed to work. She continued to sleep around with seeming abandon, sometimes even engaging in sex with her boyfriends at her home while her parents were gone away.

Finally, Don sat her down and spoke to her from a heart that felt like it would burst from the pain.

"Cathy," he said, "your mother and I have tried everything. We don't know what else to do. But we do know that you can no longer live in our home and do the things you're doing." Then Don asked his daughter to leave. He and his wife tried to assure Cathy of their love, but insisted that she either accept their help in changing her behavior or find somewhere else to live.

Cathy left the next evening. She packed a suitcase and left the house without telling her parents where she was going.

Three months later, at about one o'clock in the morning, Don was awakened by a phone call. "Daddy," the voice on the phone said, "I'm calling from the bus terminal." It was Cathy. She spoke a few rambling sentences into the phone, finally ending, "I want to come home."

Don sat up in the bed and woke his wife. "Don't go anywhere" he said to his daughter, struggling to keep his voice calm. "I'll be right there."

Don picked up his daughter at the bus station and hugged her long and tight before driving her home. He didn't interrogate her about where she'd been. He didn't lecture her about the sleepless nights she had caused. He didn't remind her of the rules she accepted in coming home. He just forgave her.

That's the kind of father we need to be—a forgiving father. Your children need to know that they can admit their faults and their wrongdoing and find forgiveness from Dad. They need to know their father won't hold grudges against them. When they mess up, they can start over again.

I tell you, I've seen the effects of an unforgiving spirit in a father. I've seen how kids whose fathers harbor resentment and bitterness over their conduct develop a low sense of self-esteem. I've observed that kids whose fathers have trouble forgiving them are often impatient themselves and unforgiving toward others. I've watched kids of unforgiving fathers rebel against home, family, and church, embittered by what they label as hypocrisy in their parents.

On the other hand, I've seen how a forgiving father can nurture a healthy sense of self-esteem and self-confidence in his child. I've noticed that forgiving fathers tend to raise kids who are forgiving and forbearing themselves. I'm convinced that a forgiving father will more easily raise kids who are honest about their faults and who quickly admit a sin or a mistake, often saving both parent and child many months or years of agony and tragedy.

That's why you should want to be a forgiving father, just like your Father is.

The Father's Forgiveness

Imagine yourself as the father of a son who has been the apple of your eye. You lavished love and attention on him from his infancy. You gave him his first bath. You taught him to ride a bicycle. You attended countless baseball games. You nursed him through sickness and cheered him through sadness. You were available to him and interested in everything he enjoyed. You provided well for him and showered him with gifts. You did everything a loving father could do for a son.

But your son took it all for granted. Most days he simply ignored you, coming to you only when he needed something, like gas money or new tennis shoes. Sometimes, he actively and willfully disobeyed you. He often deceived you. He seemed ashamed of you, and regularly treated his siblings rudely and cruelly.

How would you feel about such a son? Would you forgive him? Consider your answer carefully, because you're not the father in this story—you're the son.

Your heavenly Father has lavished you with love and grace, and you have responded much like the son in the story above. (Actually, if you're anything like me, you've done *worse* than I've depicted in this scenario.) Yet God has freely forgiven you, and he continues to do so. Amazing, isn't it? Not really. That's just the kind of Father he is. It's a part of his nature.

> As far as the east is from the west, so far has he removed our transgressions from us. As a father has compassion on his children, so the Lord has compassion on those who fear him. (Ps. 103:12–13)

> I, even I, am he who blots out your transgressions, for my own sake, and remembers your sins no more. (Isa. 43:25)

He is a forgiving Father. Though he has been wronged and his will transgressed more than any father in history, he remains ready and anxious to forgive his children. Like the waiting father in Jesus' story of the prodigal son, God not only waits but *runs* to forgive, and in his grace and generosity begins his work of forgiveness before our words of repentance are even out of our mouths (see Luke 15:11–32).

We are ill-equipped—no, we're unequipped—to be that kind of father. Our pride, fear, and frailty all get in the way. We worry that our children will misunderstand, thinking that forgiving their behavior means condoning their behavior. We can no more be a forgiving father than the man in the moon. But because the Spirit of God, our model Father, is living in us through our salvation in Christ, we can by prayer and reliance on him show his Father-image to our children. Some of the specific ways in which God has enabled us to do that include:

UNDERSTANDING FORGIVENESS

One of the barriers to forgiveness is a lack of understanding about what forgiveness is and what it does. Forgiving my children does not mean winking at their disobedience, condoning their behavior, or releasing them from punishment. Allen C. Guelzo, writing in *Christianity Today*, said:

> To forgive . . . means willingly to throw away our resentment at being wronged. This entails not just containing or restraining our resentment, but letting go of it entirely. . . .
>
> Forgiveness means more than just rolling over and playing dead. There are a few things that forgiveness is not, and these may help balance the picture. Forgiveness does not mean pardon. Forgiveness is personal: it refers to the impact an offense has on you and your need to release the resentment you feel. Pardon is legal rather than personal, concerned only with the legal status of the offense, not the relationship between the offender and the victim. And pardon, unlike forgiveness, means letting someone

off the moral hook and releasing them from the punishment they deserve. . . .

A second thing that forgiveness does not mean is excuse. . . . C. S. Lewis wrote, "There is all the difference in the world between forgiving and excusing. Forgiveness says: 'Yes, you have done this thing, but I accept your apology. I will never hold it against you, and everything between us will be exactly as it was before.' But excusing says: 'I see that you couldn't help it, or didn't mean it, you weren't really to blame.' If one was not really to blame, then there is nothing to forgive. In that sense, forgiveness and excusing are almost opposites."

If this is true, we need not be afraid that in practicing forgiveness we are somehow tolerating wrong or condoning evil. Forgiveness does not mean "ceasing to blame," but rather, "letting go of resentment."[1]

Understanding forgiveness—what it is and what it isn't—is a necessary step toward becoming a father who forgives.

RESTRAINING THE URGE TO OVERREACT

Kids can push you to your limits at times, and it can become difficult to forgive them, particularly when their every action seems intended to "push Dad's buttons." But you do a huge favor to your children—and yourself—when you resist the urge to overreact.

Whenever I was tempted to react to my kids in a harsh and unforgiving spirit, I tried to remember a conversation a friend of mine once had with a husband and wife. He was trying to help these parents deal with their rebellious son who was slowly trying to respond to their leading. At one meeting he asked them, "How did your son do last week?"

They immediately responded with all that had gone wrong on Friday. After my friend listened for fifteen minutes to what a terrible day Friday had been with their son, he asked them how

Thursday had gone. Fine. What about Wednesday? Okay. Was Tuesday a bad day? No. And, Monday, how did he act on Monday? Actually, Monday was really good.

Finally, my friend was ready to make the point. One bad day does not negate four good days of behavior. True, Friday was the pits. But couldn't they see the improvement being made on the other days and not discount them because of a setback on Friday? They began to understand how they might have overreacted, and how on the whole the son's conduct had been a marked improvement over the past.

Since love keeps no record of wrongs, you can forgive and release the bad days while focusing more on your children's successes than on their failures.

ENLISTING HELP

My wife, Dottie, has been an invaluable help to me in many ways, not the least of which have been my efforts in becoming a forgiving father.

I regularly asked Dottie to tell me when she saw me acting harshly toward our children, to point out to me when I was acting in an unforgiving way toward our kids. Believe me, she became quite adept at saying, "Josh, I think you owe Katie an apology," or "Josh, don't you think you have something to say to Heather?" It wasn't always easy to hear, but it was indispensable.

Remember, too, that if you've enlisted your kids' help in holding you accountable as a father, they too can remind you of your intention to be forgiving. They may say, "Dad, I don't think you've forgiven me for painting your sports car," or "Daddy, are you sure you've forgiven me for using your toupee for first base?"

REMEMBERING YOUR PAST

Growing up is no easy task. If we're honest, all of us dads would have to admit that when we were growing up, we made just as many (if not more) dumb and/or willful mistakes as our own children do now. We had bad days. We were grumpy. We were mischievous—sometimes downright devilish! There were times when we just plain rebelled.

Never did we stop to think that God might have a way of gaining vengeance on our parents' behalf by giving us children of our own that are as mischievous and rebellious as *we* were!

Forgiveness is easier if we keep a close handle on our own foibles and failures—not only those of our childhood but those of our more recent past, as well. When your son is late for curfew, for example, it might help to ask yourself if you've been late for any appointment this week yourself. (You may still need to attach a penalty to the behavior for teaching purposes, of course, but remembering your past may nonetheless help foster a forgiving spirit in you.) If your daughter gets a speeding ticket, remembering your last moving violation may help you more readily communicate forgiveness to her.

PRACTICING FORGIVENESS

Yes, be the kind of father who forgives his kids no matter how "big" their transgression. But also be the kind of father who forgives his kids for the "small" things. It's been my experience that "practicing" forgiveness in the small, everyday things helps to prepare a father to show forgiveness in the face of a major crisis.

Each day has multiple opportunities to practice forgiveness. For example, if a child spoke disrespectfully to me or to Dottie, I'd correct the behavior and then consciously practice forgiveness. If the child responded positively to the correction, I'd often smile and say, "You're forgiven." (I tried never to say, "Oh, that's okay," or "No problem," because I wanted to focus on communicating forgiveness, not approval of the behavior).

Or, to use another example, if a child broke curfew, I'd use that relatively minor incident to practice my "forgiveness skills." Being careful not to overreact, I'd attach an appropriate penalty to the misbehavior (such as, "I think your curfew will be an hour earlier for the next month") and then would communicate my forgiveness.

Such seemingly "small" opportunities to practice forgiveness not only helped me (with God's help) to communicate a forgiving spirit to my children. They also kept me "in shape" for more difficult moments, when crises hit, when it was harder—and more necessary—to forgive.

DOING A "MAGNET CHECK"

Dick Day, who coauthored *How to Be a Hero to Your Kids* with me, offered the following counsel, which I think applies to our discussion in this chapter:

> When I start feeling tension with my children, I find that it's best to try to step back and see them as God sees them; persons of infinite worth. This helps put me in an accepting and forgiving mode even when the situation may call for discipline. I can still affirm them and forgive them even as I deal with their behavior.
>
> I call this stepping-back process a "magnet check." When two magnets are separated and not in the same magnetic field, they have no influence on each other. But if you place two magnets within the *same* magnetic field, they will do one of two things: become attracted to each other or repel each other.
>
> Our human emotions make us very much like magnets. You don't have magnetic powers, but you do have emotions, and so does your child. Living together as a family puts you and your kids in the same "emotional field," and when that happens, there is a result similar to placing magnets close to one another. One of two things happens: you either come together with your child, or you react to each other and push each other away.
>
> Whenever I find myself in a tense situation with my children, I ask myself some hard questions: "Why is our relationship under stress? Why am I reacting to my child? Why is my child reacting to me?" When things

get tense—or worse—in your family, you can count on it: somebody's security is being threatened and your acceptance of the child is also in jeopardy.[2]

Keep in mind, of course, that doing magnet checks is *your* responsibility, not your child's. As an adult, you are the one who should be able to step back—outside the situation—and be able to see what's happening. Then you can bring any anger or resentment you may have under control and, if warranted, express forgiveness or ask for it, which brings us to our next point . . .

ASKING FOR FORGIVENESS YOURSELF

When I was first writing this chapter, I sat my sixteen-year-old daughter Katie down and told her I needed her help with it. "Can you think of a time," I asked her, "when I hurt you, offended you, and I didn't come back and ask you to forgive me?"

She sat in silence for what seemed like five or six minutes, thinking. I could almost imagine wheels turning inside her head as she ran through a mental catalog of all the hasty, thoughtless, and cruel things I had said and done in sixteen years as her father. I imagined that by this time, she was mentally sorting through dozens of incidents, trying to pick the one that was just right, the one that portrayed me in the worst possible light. Finally, I couldn't take the suspense anymore. Katie still hadn't said a word. So, trying to bring the agonizing silence to an end, I said, "Honey, just anything."

She smiled. "Well, Daddy," she said, "this might be good for *you*, but it won't be good for your book." I had a sudden thought that she was about to relate something so horrifying it couldn't even be printed. Then she shrugged her shoulders and said, "I can't think of anything."

What a relief! And—(I'm sure my wife would add)—how surprising!

Now, I'm not suggesting that I compiled a perfect record as a father. I'm sure there were times when I should have asked for

Katie's forgiveness and didn't. But at sixteen years of age, Katie couldn't think of any and, to be honest, neither could I. If there *were* any, I'd have done my best to take care of it right away.

The ability to admit mistakes and ask forgiveness is apparently rare among Christian parents. A survey of churched kids revealed that 37 percent of the kids surveyed—more than one in three—say they seldom or never hear their parents admit to being wrong or having done wrong. Presumably, even fewer ask for forgiveness from their children.

No wonder our kids have trouble admitting their mistakes! No wonder they have trouble identifying with their parents! No wonder they struggle with self-esteem—their parents are apparently perfect!

How blessed is the child whose father is patient with his sins and quick to forgive, whose father never holds his past failures over his head like a sword. Such a father can more readily and more richly instill wisdom, godliness, and maturity in his children. Such a father can more readily and more richly foster a sense of self-esteem and self-confidence in his kids. Such a father can more readily and more richly train children who are quick to admit their mistakes, and quick to repent of their sins. Such a father can more readily and more richly raise children who are themselves forgiving and patient toward others. Such a father can more readily and more richly reflect the image of his Father in heaven . . . and in so doing, attract his children to the model Father as well.

For Reflection, Discussion, and Action

1. To what degree have you been a forgiving father in the past? Circle the statement below that most accurately reflects your past practice:

   I have been a forgiving father.
   I have been hesitant to forgive.
   I have sometimes communicated forgiveness to my kids.
   I have seldom communicated forgiveness to my kids.
   I have never communicated forgiveness to my kids.

2. In the space provided below, describe if and how forgiveness happened in the home in which you grew up. What is similar in your home today? What has changed?

   _____

   _____

   _____

   _____

3. What can you do this week to more effectively communicate forgiveness to your children? Be specific, and list ideas below:

   _____

   _____

   _____

   _____

4. Are there any situations you need to ask forgiveness for from your kids? If so, what are they, and when will you ask?

   _____

   _____

   _____

   _____

CHAPTER 12

The Father and Respect

This story is told of Archbishop Tillotson, when he was Dean of Canterbury, a position of great power and prestige. He was in his home one afternoon when a caller appeared at the door.

One of the dean's servants answered the ring and found a somewhat bedraggled old man, a common Yorkshireman, who asked if "John Tillotson" were home. The servant, shocked by the old man's insolence at thus addressing the esteemed Dean of Canterbury, upbraided the visitor and drove him away from the house, dusting his hands at the stranger's departure as though he had just taken out the garbage.

The dean, however, had recognized the stranger's voice from inside the house and ran to the door just as the servant was closing it. He flung the door open and cried out, to the astonishment of the servants, "It is my beloved father!"

The respected churchman ran up the path to where his father had stopped, fell on his knees, and asked his father's blessing.

Though Dean Tillotson had risen to a position of great honor in the church, he nonetheless loved and respected his Yorkshireman father, common and ordinary though he may have appeared. The dean's show of respect not only reflected his own character but hinted at his father's character as well. That's the kind of child we want to raise. That's the kind of fathers we want to be.

We want to earn the respect of our children. We want them to respect us. We want them to respect their mother. We want them to respect their elders. We want them to respect authority. We want them to respect themselves.

Such an ideal is not unrealistic. I'm convinced it's possible. But I believe the reason this kind of respect is so rare today is because such kids are, to a large extent, products of the first nine father qualities we've discussed in this book. Fathers only earn the respect of their wives and children by modeling love, acceptance, purity, truth, faithfulness, friendship, forgiveness, and so on. Each of these qualities demonstrates a father's respect and demonstrates that he is worthy of respect.

Respect flows to—and from—a father who is like the Father.

The Father Figure

The Bible abounds with exhortations to respect others. Children are enjoined to respect parents. The Bible commands us to "Honor your father and your mother" (Exod. 20:12). We are instructed to "show respect for the elderly" (Lev. 19:32). We are told to "submit . . . to the governing authorities" (Rom. 13:1). Paul advised Timothy that "the elders who direct the affairs of the church well are worthy of double honor" (1 Tim. 5:17).

The Bible commands respect because respecting others is right. There is something respectable about each of us that comes from the very nature of God himself. "God is Spirit," and in him is "life," the Bible says (John 4:24; John 1:4). It is that part of his nature that every human being shares, for "the LORD God . . . breathed into his nostrils the breath [the ruach, 'spirit'] of life, and the man became a living being" (Gen. 2:7). Humans are made in the image of God (Gen. 1:26–27). We are immortal spirits, created with dignity and purpose. Every human being, therefore, is worthy of respect because he or she is a reflection of the God who gives life and breath to all people.

In addition to a basic respect for every human being, we are commanded to respect and obey those in authority over us, "for there is no authority except from God, and those which exist are established by God" (Rom. 13:1, NASB). Respect for civil rulers and church leaders is an acknowledgment of God's authority over all.

Amazingly, God not only *commands* respect from us and among us, he also *shows* us respect. He created us "in his image." Because of that, he treats us with dignity, far more respectfully than we deserve:

> What is man that you are mindful of him, and the son of man that you care for him? You made him a little lower than the heavenly beings and crowned him with glory and honor. (Ps. 8:4–5)

God is a respectful Father. He is also a Father who is worthy of the highest respect. That's the kind of father I want to be. Oh, I know I'm not—nor will I ever be—worthy of respect as he is. He is holy and almighty; I am sinful and weak. But through the sacrifice of his Son and the work of his Holy Spirit, I can display his image in my ministry as a father to my children. That requires dependence on him through attention to prayer and the Word. It is also aided by attention to the following areas or skills:

SHOWING RESPECT

How do you treat your own parents? How do you speak about others in the presence of young people? Do you show respect for your spouse? Your superiors? Leaders in the church? Coworkers? Traffic laws? City ordinances? God's creation?

One of the keys to becoming a father who is worthy of respect is being a father who shows respect, just as God the Father not only commands respect but shows it to us, as well. Modeling respectful attitudes and actions to the youth in your life will show them in concrete ways what respect looks and sounds like.

Showing respect also includes treating your own kids with respect. Some adults consider respect to be a one-way street, but *children* are made in the image of God, too. I've seen fathers browbeat their kids after a poor performance at a sporting event. I've seen them roll their eyes at a child's innocent statement. I've seen them insult their kids or call them names. I've seen them talk to a seventeen-year-old son as if he were six.

The road to respect begins at our feet, dads. It begins with seeing our kids through God's eyes and treating them with honor. It means asking for our kids' opinions, then listening when they respond. It means saying "please" and "thank you" to our kids, just as we would to anyone else. It means displaying respect for everyone—even our own children—and treating them like the children of God they are.

DEFINING RESPECT

Some kids have been told to act respectfully without ever understanding what respect is. Their parents have never defined it for them.

Defining respect includes making your kids aware of the biblical commands to respect all human beings, particularly parents, elders, and governmental and church authorities. It can also include explaining manners—such as addressing elders as "sir" and "ma'am," or opening the door for someone—as ways of communicating respect to other people.

I recall one occasion when Sean rode with me to the shopping center. The two of us were engrossed in conversation as we arrived at the parking lot, and I parked the car rather hurriedly. I was halfway out of the car when I noticed I'd parked almost right in the center of two parking places instead of between the lines for one. For a second, I was tempted just to leave the car where it was because we were in a bit of a hurry. But then I told myself, "No, this could mean somebody else would have to walk farther because they can't find a parking place. What kind of role modeling is that for your son?"

I asked Sean to stay put in his seat. As I parked the car once more, I realized the opportunity to do a little teaching.

"Son," I said, "do you know why I'm backing up?"

"Why, Dad?" he asked.

"Well," I said, "you can see I didn't do a very good job of parking. In fact, I took up two places. It would be rude to leave the car parked like this. Somebody else might not be able to find a place, and they'd have to walk a lot farther to get into the store."

I used that opportunity to define respect for my son and to help him understand what respectful behavior looks like.

FOSTERING SELF-RESPECT

A healthy respect toward others begins with self-respect. The young person who doesn't respect himself or herself will find it difficult to respect Mom and Dad, teachers, pastors, or anyone else. Fathers can help foster self-respect within their kids by communicating the following things:

I respect you because you're created in the image of God. It's true that sin has marred and dimmed that image. Nevertheless, every child is worthy of respect because he or she reflects the image of God.

I respect you because you are a fellow member (or potential member) of God's eternal family. Christians are affirmed by the apostle Paul as "God's workmanship" (Eph. 2:10). The word Paul used for "workmanship" in that verse is *poiema*, a word which was distinctly used to refer to precious works of art (and from which we get our English word "poem"). In other words, your child is God's "poem," his masterpiece, his precious work of art.

I respect you because you enrich my life. Psalm 127:3 says that children are a special gift from a loving heavenly Father. Acknowledging that children enrich our lives is not a lofty, abstract truth. They, more than anyone else, can challenge us to become the best person we can be through God's grace. Yes, children learn from us, but they also teach us. You know what I was telling Sean on that trip to the shopping center I mentioned earlier, when I parked so badly? I was saying, "Sean, you're really special to me, and I want you to learn from this experience just like I'm learning from it myself. I want you to know that I count it a privilege to be your dad. I'm one of the luckiest men in the world." (No wonder he failed to notice my poor driving!)

I respect you because of your uniqueness, your personality, your talents, and your gifts. Every human being—young or old—needs to feel a sense of belonging, a sense of worthiness, and a sense of competence. Listen to what one young woman had to say of her parents:

> When I first began to think about what [my parents] did right, their appreciation for us as individuals with different gifts stood out most in my mind.
>
> My sister and I did well academically, enjoying things like memorizing and writing essays. Our two brothers were into writing, acting, art, poetry. They enjoyed creating. All of us were encouraged to learn, to develop good study habits, to do well in school. At the same time, we felt great freedom and lack of pressure because of our parents' refusal to place value judgments on our abilities. [My parents] were study oriented, for example, yet they accepted the boys' creative gifts with as much praise and encouragement as any academic achievement.[1]

That kind of attitude, when communicated to children, can contribute significantly to healthy attitudes of self-respect.

DEMANDING RESPECT FOR YOUR WIFE

Many years ago, when our oldest daughter Kelly was about eleven years old, she and Dottie went through a difficult period in which they just grated on each other. Kelly began "sassing" her mother and talking rather disrespectfully to her.

After observing this a few times, I decided that enough was enough. I grabbed Kelly by the shoulders, gently swung her around, looked her in the eye and said, "Young lady, you might talk to your *mother* that way, but I will never let you talk to my *wife* that way! I love this woman, and I will not only protect her from people *outside* the family, I will also protect her from you kids. Don't ever talk to my wife that way again!"

Kelly blinked, mumbled something, and walked away. But the results of my little speech were immediate. The next time she started to make some smart remark to Dottie, she caught herself, looked at me, and said, "Oh, I can't talk to your wife that way, can I?"

"No, Kelly, you can't," I replied with a twinkle in my eye.

Children learn respect in the home, of course, and to allow them to speak disrespectfully to their mother would teach the opposite of what I want them to learn.

INSISTING ON RESPECT BETWEEN SIBLINGS

Brothers and sisters can be best friends, bitter enemies, or both, depending on the circumstance, their ages, the time of day, or their moods. Siblings can be surprisingly loving toward each other, and they can also be shockingly cruel.

Differences and disagreements may be inevitable among brothers and sisters, but disrespect need not be tolerated. A wise father will draw the line at name-calling, insults, and cruel teasing, explaining that these do not meet biblical standards for God's people. Dr. James Dobson offers the boundaries of respect he drew in his own family:

1. Neither child is ever allowed to make fun of the other in a destructive way. Period!
2. Each child's room (or portion of the room, if siblings share a room) is his private territory.
3. The older child is not permitted to tease the younger child.
4. The younger child is not permitted to harass the older child.

5. The children are not required to play with each other when they prefer to be alone or with friends.

6. We mediate any genuine conflict as quickly as possible, being careful to always show impartiality and extreme fairness.[2]

SEIZING TEACHABLE MOMENTS

Effective fathers look for every opportunity to impart wisdom and insight, seize those teachable moments, and wring every drop of possibility out of it.

Directed conversations at the evening meal, for example, can stimulate thinking and implant seeds of truth in your kids. (This assumes, of course, that your family eats dinner together regularly. If you don't, *why not?* Such moments—with the television off—provide golden opportunities for discussing respectful behavior. If your family doesn't dine together regularly, consider making it a standard procedure again.)

Take advantage of the drive to the mall or time spent working with a child on a project to discuss why respect is important. Don't be afraid to ask your child how you can do better at showing respect for him or her. You may also gently suggest one or two ways in which your child's behavior can become more respectful.

Try taking each child out on a "date," as mentioned earlier in this book, to teach him or her how to treat a member of the opposite sex with respect and how to accept respectful gestures. When you witness a child being rude to his mother in the supermarket, use that incident to spark conversation with your teen on the way home. Rather than shying away from television shows that depict kids being rude to parents, tune in to such shows with the purpose of asking your teens during the commercials if disrespectful behavior makes the character funny, attractive, or successful (and be prepared for honest answers).

To be a father like your Father in heaven, you need to know that a father who *shows* respect will also *earn* respect. This kind of father is more likely to raise kids who respect authority, who respect themselves, who respect their siblings and their peers. He's the kind of father that is more likely to raise daughters who may someday say, "I want to marry someone who's like my daddy, someone I can admire and respect, " or sons who may someday say, "I want to be just like you, Dad." This kind of father is more likely to raise kids who earn the respect of their friends, families, coworkers, employers, and—someday—their own children, too.

That's the kind of father we all want to be. And, with God's help, that's the kind of father we will be.

For Reflection, Discussion, and Action

1. Rank the sections of this chapter according to which strategy you consider to be the most urgent and important in your family at this time (rank them 1–6, with "1" being the area that needs the most attention):

___ Showing respect

___ Defining respect

___ Fostering self-respect

___ Demanding respect for your wife

___ Insisting on respect between siblings

___ Seizing teachable moments

2. In the space provided below, list ways that you can do a better job of showing respect to others (your parents, your wife, your superiors, leaders in the church):

_____

_____

_____

_____

_____

_____

_____

3. In the space provided below, list ways that you can do a better job of showing respect to your children:

_____

_____

_____

_____

_____

_____

_____

*4. List three concrete steps you plan to take this week to foster respectful attitudes and actions in both yourself and in your children:

- _____

  _____

  _____

- _____

  _____

  _____

- _____

  _____

  _____

Next, transform these steps to specific, measurable actions, and then transfer them to your daily calendar.

CHAPTER 13
A Father after God's Own Heart

Samuel, God's prophet, did as he was instructed. He visited the home of Jesse, a shepherd of Bethlehem, to examine Jesse's sons like a general inspecting his troops. One of them, the Lord had told him, was God's choice to be king of Israel.

He saw Jesse's son Eliab first and thought, "This must be the one. Look at him! He's a man's man. He's got everything going for him—strength, size, wits, good looks." But God said, "Nope. He's not the one I have in mind."

Samuel's gaze next fell upon Abinadab, and the prophet thought he could understand God's reasoning. "Not as big as Eliab, but he's one cool customer, that's obvious. I could see him leading troops into battle without a trace of fear on his face." God said, "Keep the line moving, Samuel. You don't have all day."

So Samuel turned to Jesse's next son, Shammah, sensing the Lord's answer before he even heard it: "Not this one either."

Samuel reviewed all seven sons that Jesse had proudly displayed to the Lord's prophet, and God answered no to each one. Samuel began to wonder, "Lord, have you and I gotten our wires crossed? You *did* say Jesse of Bethlehem, didn't you?"

Finally, sure that he was in the right place, Samuel asked, "Jesse, are these all the sons you have?"

The confused father answered with a shrug and a wave of his hand. "There's still the youngest," he answered, "but he is tending the sheep."

"Send for him," Samuel said with the authority that only a prophet of God could summon.

So Jesse sent for his youngest son, David.

When Samuel saw the boy approaching, he felt a sensation like a spark travel through his body, and he felt (more than heard) the Lord say, "Rise and anoint him; he is the one." That day, Samuel anointed David as the next king of Israel.

The new king was by no means an obvious choice. His older brothers were proven warriors, tested leaders. They were each bigger, stronger, and more learned than the one God had chosen to be king. But David's qualification had been announced much earlier, before King Saul had subdued both the Philistines and the Amalekites, before Saul had angered the Lord's prophet and disobeyed God at Gilgal. Samuel told the king that God had already sought out "a man after his own heart and appointed him leader of his people" (1 Sam. 13:14).

David did not become king because of his size, his military prowess, or even his intelligence. He became king because he was a man after God's own heart. He was qualified to lead Israel because of his relationship—his kinship—with God.

A man after God's own heart. That's the kind of man I want to be. That's the kind of father I want to be: a father after God's own heart. I want to model the Father's heart to my children—his unconditional love and acceptance. I want to reflect his holiness and purity. I want to show myself to be a truthful and trustworthy father, a comfort and a refuge to my children, just as he is to his children. I want to be a friend to my children, as he is; to provide godly discipline for my children; to forgive the way he forgives. I want my children to respect me, and I want them to earn the respect of others.

Fathering is a difficult and complex task for any generation, but Jerry Adler, writing in *Newsweek*, suggests that "in a single generation, fatherhood (like motherhood) has gotten twice as hard."[1] He cites the increased demands and expectations that society places upon fathers these days.

Certainly, fatherhood in the twenty-first century is a challenge that can tax a man's resources and stretch his imagination to the limit. But if you've determined to be a father after God's own heart, you are not limited by your own resources or your own imagination. As a matter of fact, you are not limited at all, because God is your resource, and he is willing and able to supply "all your needs according to his glorious riches in Christ Jesus" (Phil. 4:19). And he will do so more and more as you face your task of fathering with true biblical optimism.

The Right Attitude

God's Word teaches us that the way a man "thinketh in his heart, so is he" (Prov. 23:7, KJV). Your mental attitude sets you up to either move forward optimistically, like a mighty vessel plowing through the angry waves of the ocean, or to hesitate, seeing every problem as an enemy trying to torpedo your ship. A positive mental attitude is crucial for handling the unique circumstances and personal limitations that may come your way in fathering.

If you haven't done so yet, decide now that you are going to face fathering with true biblical optimism. The apostle Paul said, "I can do everything through him who gives me strength" (Phil. 4:13). The "everything" of that statement includes being an effective, godly dad in demanding situations.

The Bible says that our loving Father oversees every aspect of our lives. He knows our circumstances, and he wants to use those very situations to strengthen us and stimulate us to the full stature of men of God. So whatever your roadblocks, limitations, or difficulties, consider them opportunities for growth. It is my conviction that fathering is one of the key ways the Lord brings men to maturity. That's reason enough to be optimistic.

Often our mental attitude is not as positive as it could be because we think of parenting in terms of *my* responsibility, *my* skills, *my* knowledge. We lose sight of the Lord's commitment to participate in every facet of our lives. But when we think in terms of seeking *his* wisdom, *his* strength, *his* love, *his* patience, and *his* compassion, our perspective changes. Only his Spirit can create the qualities and skills we need in order to become fathers after his heart. Our part is to walk with him through the fathering experience, daily inviting and anticipating his active, faithful participation.

Let's summarize these thoughts in four statements: (1) your positive, mental attitude greatly enhances your effectiveness as a dad; (2) fathering is an opportunity for significant growth in your life; (3) the challenges of fathering lead you to discover the vastness and reality of God's nature and resources for your own life; and (4) it's possible to be a father after the Father's heart!

Face Up to Your Special Challenges

Being a father can be incredibly hard work. It may even be painful. But the difficulty and pain of fatherhood is not something to fear. No matter what special challenges you may face, no matter what your childhood was like, no matter what your weaknesses may be, you can experience God's enabling power to show his image—the Father's image—in and through you.

Many dads face situations that are so intense and demanding that they merit discussion here. You may find yourself in a difficult situation because of choices you made. You may be overwhelmed by circumstances beyond your control. Either way, to be an effective father, you'll want to face the problem honestly and make any changes that are necessary.

THE OVERWORKED DAD

In our grandfather's generation, men labored physically. Today, however, a man's labor is much more likely to be mentally and emotionally demanding. He faces time deadlines, the pressures of filling weekly or monthly quotas, the mental stresses associated with an electronic world and a fast-paced life. If you're like many dads, you probably find yourself coming home at the end of a workday mentally and emotionally exhausted, still thinking about what went on that day and what will happen tomorrow. Plus, many of us work well beyond the forty-hour week. In many cases, we leave ourselves limited reserves for parenting.

In addition to our jobs, most of us have other interests that compete with our families for our time. Sports, hobbies, home maintenance, church activities, community involvement, and a host of other activities vie for our attention.

If you're an overcommitted dad, your challenge is twofold:

First, you need to reevaluate your personality and priorities. Perhaps you feel more significant or even more secure if you're busy. Are you overcommitted because you want it that way? Or have you failed to set priorities to determine (from a Christian perspective) what should be most significant in your life? You may be uncomfortable grappling with these questions. They may even be threatening to you. But it's important to realize that ignoring these questions may cause irreparable damage in your relationship with your children.

A man's priorities are put to the test when he's offered a lucrative job advancement which conflicts with the needs of family members. Ray was such a man. At a men's retreat, he related the following incident:

> The company vice president called me into his office and told me I was set to be promoted to a new position. It would mean that our family would relocate to another city, and I would be given additional responsibilities. Initially I was thrilled because I never could resist a new challenge.
>
> But as with every important decision I've been faced with, I began to seek God's direction. When I committed this opportunity to him, he helped me see that it would

not be healthy for our family. My relationship with my two sons is so fulfilling that I knew I couldn't give it second place to a job.

It was hard to decline the promotion, knowing I might not get another chance like this again. But in my heart I knew I'd made the right choice.

That's a man after God's own heart! Ray's decision reflected godly priorities, and he is still reaping the reward.

The second challenge for the busy dad is to work smart. For example, Neil is a salesman who travels within his state. He frequently has to be away from home Monday through Friday. When Neil has a week like that, he makes sure that Saturday is family day. His children look forward to that day, knowing they'll have their dad's full attention.

The smart dad who is busy looks for ways to make the maximum use of briefer time periods. A twenty-minute walk with your daughter can accomplish much if you give her your full attention during that time. Twenty minutes of one-on-one basketball in the driveway with your son before dinner can be as good for that relationship as it is for your heart and waistline. A regular family dinner time—with the TV and telephone off—can be a haven of warm, cheerful conversation for every family member.

It may take extra effort, it may mean shifting some priorities, but a busy dad can still be a father after God's own heart.

THE DIVORCED DAD

Perhaps your fathering has been affected by a divorce. This can weaken—sometimes sever—the relationship between father and child. In the majority of cases, the children continue to live with their mother. If a divorced mom is bitter or hostile toward the children's father, that father's relationship with the children can be strained even further. Many dads find it difficult to maintain a meaningful relationship with their children when it can only be maintained through infrequent contacts.

A crucial warning for divorced dads and moms: never put your children in the middle of your problems. If one parent expresses resentment toward the other parent, the child is likely to reflect the same resentment.

My friend Dick Day, a family, marriage and child counselor, once told me how a divorced mother came for counseling about her thirteen-year-old daughter. The dad had left the family when the mom was pregnant with this girl, and now the teen was extremely bitter toward her father. Dick asked the mother how much time the daughter had spent with her dad in the past thirteen years. She estimated about two months. Dick immediately confronted the mother: "The feelings your daughter has toward her father could not have come from those two months of exposure to him. I suspect that those feelings toward her dad have come from you, not her experience."

The woman went home to think about it, then returned the following week. "You're right," she told Dick. "I've been force-feeding my own resentment to my daughter, and it's been harmful to her. I've got to be more positive about her father."

I know many divorced dads who've accepted the challenge, weathered the trying times, and continued to have significant positive influence on their children. These dads think and act with the Father's insight and wisdom.

Wise divorced dads plan thoughtfully and creatively. Rex is such a man. He has two daughters. One was eleven and the other was thirteen when the divorce occurred. Even though Rex had to work through his own emotional pain, he consistently affirmed his love and commitment to the girls—nothing spectacular, just genuine fatherly love and care. When they were with him on Saturdays, he spent time working together with them and doing the things they liked. After a while, his ex-wife realized that she couldn't care for their children, so they went to live with Rex, who by this time had remarried. Today, both girls have more stable lives because of a dad who wouldn't quit when the going got tough.

Divorced dads can better nourish their children if they themselves are living healthy, fulfilled lives. When a man's life is filled with emptiness, boredom, or resentment, these are certain to seep out and infect those around him. The man who has personal challenges, who maintains close personal friendships through support groups, and who focuses his energy on caring for others will be a more positive model for his children to follow.

THE STEPDAD

In recent years, the number of remarried parents and "blended families" has soared. When this book was first released, over 40 percent of all marriages in the U.S. involved a remarriage of one or both parties.[2] Today, according to research cited by Focus on the Family, "approximately 1,300 new stepfamilies are formed every day in the U.S., and it's predicted that by 2010 there will be more stepfamilies in the U.S. than any other type of family."[3] This is happening fast, and the future is sure to be filled with the ramifications.

Being a father is tough enough; being a stepdad can be even tougher. Your stepchild may resent your infringing on what he feels is his personal territory—his mother. He perceives you as someone vying for his mother's attention and affection. He also will likely resent your efforts to give leadership in his life. He may wonder how much authority you legitimately have over him because you're not really his dad. And even if he likes you, he is caught in a loyalty crisis. To accept you or be friendly to you may seem to him like a betrayal of his own father.

Establishing a good, fruitful relationship as a stepdad is not an overnight process. I've noticed, however, that the stepdad who is willing to "go the second mile" may have the joy of ministering to the child in a powerful way. I have also observed stepparent-child relationships that have been strong, warm, and lasting. I'd like to share some general guidelines to help you as a stepdad.

Remember that blending takes time. Children need time to sort out their feelings and become open to a relationship with you. If you move too quickly into the relationship, or endeavor to establish strong authority over the child, he will likely back away. Give the child time to get to know you, to establish a trust relationship, to work through his turbulent feelings.

In many blended family situations, the following sequence unfolds:

1. *Initial acceptance by the child:* "I like him; marry him." The woman's kids may feel that whatever makes Mom happy is fine.

2. *The end of the honeymoon for the child:* "I don't like you! You're not my dad! I won't do what you ask me to do!" It's important that you not be discouraged or overwhelmed at this stage. Remember that the child may have many unclear emotions stirring within him. You may be the object of his anger toward his natural father. Or he may be testing you to see if you really care about him. Your continued compassion, patience, and openness are likely to win out in the end.

3. *Acceptance by the child on a tested, confident basis:* The child knows you really care about him as a person, no matter what he does or whose child he is.

The third and final stage above may take weeks or months. In some cases, it may even take years. But the rewards of fatherhood await a stepfather after God's own heart, just as they do a father.

THE DEFICIENT DAD

All of us belong to this group, though we may not want to admit it. Each of us enters fatherhood with deficiencies of one kind or another. But God can conquer—and even use—all our imperfections, inadequacies, and limitations to make us fathers after the Father's own heart.

Some men have *personality limitations* that reduce their fathering effectiveness. For example, as long as Al can remember, he has had a deep-rooted anger that leaks out in both verbal and nonverbal communication. Karl feels defeated because he can never say no to anyone and puts his family second to everyone else's wants. He suffers from a lot of guilt. Paul grew up being the community wimp and has always felt ashamed that he isn't more courageous.

Other men have *skill limitations*. They honestly don't know how to be competent fathers. Mark is an outstanding CPA and highly respected by his peers, but talk to him about his children, and his face drops. "I think I'm blowing it, and I don't know what to do," he sighs.

One common lament I've heard during the many parenting seminars I've conducted over the years is, "I wish I'd learned these things when our children were younger. I've done so many dumb things."

One reason why many men lack fathering skills is because they didn't have a positive model to follow. Many men grew up in fatherless homes. Others grew up in homes where dad was largely an absent family member because of work, outside interests, or neglect, and our impersonal society greatly reduces the opportunity for children to find adult role models outside the home. Many fathers were never shown what good fathering was all about. My prayer is that this book will help to fill that void.

Limitations Are Growth Opportunities

Let's face it honestly: we all have personal limitations. The Christian life is a life of growth. It is God's call to each of us to find new liberation from enslaving sins and habit patterns that have robbed us of joy and fruitfulness. If we are honest with ourselves, we must admit that our weaknesses and failures in fathering are calling us to deal with personal growth issues. We can deny them, or we can see them as invitations to grow into the godly men, husbands, and fathers God has called us to be.

I believe that life is a special gift from our loving Father. God's redemption offered through Jesus Christ is his clear signal that he wants to accomplish a powerful transformation within us. His resources are readily available. All he wants is our response to him as he calls us to his side where he can love, instruct, enrich, free, and bless us. Parenting is one practical setting in which he can work this out.

You have your special set of circumstances, your unique strengths and weaknesses. Let fathering be that life situation in which you commit yourself to becoming the man of God the Lord has called you to be. Not only will your own life become more satisfying, but you will also pass on to your sons and daughters a genuine hunger and thirst for righteousness. And this would indeed be the greatest gift you could ever leave them.

Whether you know it or not, the ten fatherhood traits I've discussed in this book already exist in you if you have been born of the Spirit (John 3:8, 2 Thess. 2:13). Through prayer, practice, and growing in Christ, each of these qualities can be refined and released in your relationship with your children. By relying on him day by day, you can be a father like your Father in heaven.

For Reflection, Discussion, and Action

1. Assess your general attitude toward the challenges of fathering your kids. Is it positive, negative, or somewhere in between? Explain the reason for your answer.

   _____

   _____

   _____

   _____

2. How would your wife assess your attitude toward the challenges of fathering your kids? Explain your answer.

   _____

   _____

   _____

3. Write out and memorize a completion for this statement: "Being a loving, involved dad to my kids is a positive experience for me because . . ."

   _____

   _____

   _____

*4. What two concepts stood out most to you from this chapter? Explain why they caught your attention and what action you intend to take to integrate them into your life.

   _____

   _____

   _____

   _____

*5. Find a quiet place and invest ten to twenty minutes writing out a completion to this statement: "As a result of reading, thinking about, and discussing this book, I intend to...." Be as specific and thorough as possible. Then share what you've written with your group. When all have shared, join together in prayer that God will help you implement the action points you've written. If you are not in a group, share what you've written with your wife or with a trusted friend.

_____

_____

_____

_____

_____

_____

_____

_____

_____

_____

_____

_____

_____

_____

_____

6. Which of the ten fathering qualities discussed in this book is strongest in your life? Which need more cultivation? Pray for God's power to help you grow in each quality.

_____

_____

_____

_____

_____

_____

60 FUN THINGS A DAD CAN DO WITH HIS KIDS

1. Have a "Date with Dad" once every three months with each of your children.

2. Hold a Sunday afternoon family board games marathon.

3. Take a walk through the neighborhood at Christmas to see the lights.

4. Do a basic home or car repair job together.

5. Cook up a special meal for Mom. Have the kids make menus, and everyone serves as a waiter or waitress. (Then clean up afterward!)

6. Go to breakfast together. Let your child order for you.

7. Build a model together, but let your child do most of the actual work.

8. Take a nature hike.

9. Go camping overnight or for the full weekend.

10. Bake a major batch of chocolate chip cookies to distribute to your child's friends.

11. Do photo shoots together on walks, at the zoo, around the house, and so forth. Select photos and work together on a scrapbook.

12. Select key Scripture verses and memorize them together, discussing what each verse means to you. Reward each other with frozen yogurt each time you both can quote ten new verses word-perfect.

13. Have a croquet or badminton tournament in your backyard.

14. Play a video game together.

15. Work on a computer together.

16. Go to your child's athletic or special activities. Encourage and praise (but don't be a pushy "Little League Parent").

17. Say, "I want to be praying for you this week. What's on your mind? What would you like me to pray about?"

18. Design and plant a flower garden together.

19. Make a basket of fresh fruit, breads, gourmet crackers, and canned goods, then leave it on the porch of a needy family.

20. Ask, "What's the best thing that happened to you today?"

21. Ask your children to pray for you.

22. Put together a surprise "This Is Your Life" program for Mom or for the grandparents.

23. Tell your kids why you love their mother. Have them tell you why they love her, Then get a piece of poster board and join the kids in writing all these reasons on a giant greeting card with crayon. Have the kids decorate and deliver the card to Mom.

24. Join with one or two other families for a family skit and talent night, with everyone participating. Rent a video camera to record the event for posterity.

25. At dinner, have everyone share "My Most Embarrassing Moment."

26. With 3 x 5 cards, staple together a handmade coupon book for each child. Each coupon entitles them to a one-on-one date with Dad for ice cream, a ball game, bowling or roller skating, a game of their choice, pizza, whatever. (Suggested rule: Limit one coupon per month per child.)

27. Read through a book of the Bible together, discussing it as you go.

28. Go to a local, state, or national museum.

29. Pick out a cologne for Mom that you all like.

30. Find an apple or cherry orchard and arrange a day of fruit picking with your kids.

31. Go shopping for your and their clothes together.

32. Check your city for free outdoor concerts or plays in the park. Fix a picnic and make an evening of it.

33. Take a trip to the library. Get each child a library card and help them discover the world of good books.

34. Buy or rent an aerobics video and work out together.

35. Go to plays and concerts staged by local colleges and universities.

36. Go for a series of family bike rides.

37. Go fly a kite together.

38. Walk to construction sites and watch the progress on a building, house, or road.

39. If your children have surviving grandparents, have a "Grandparents Appreciation Day" with homemade cards, crafts, and goodies made by you and the kids. Then do the same for Mom, then for a neighbor or friend, then for your pastor or youth pastor.

40. Put together a jigsaw puzzle.

41. After family dinner, back the chairs away from the table and play "Concentration," that favorite old parlor game where players number off, then slap knees twice, clap hands twice, and call out their number and someone else's number as they snap their fingers. Then everyone pitches in to clean up the kitchen. The winner gets to choose his task.

42. Get on the floor and watch your young child's favorite TV program with him.

43. Take your kids with you to pick flowers from the garden, and assemble a bouquet for Mom or another special person.

44. By yourself, pick flowers and assemble a bouquet for your daughter.

45. Build a bookshelf or soap box racer with your son.

46. Have a candlelight night. Turn out all the lights, light candles and build a fire, pop popcorn, and sit around telling favorite stories.

47. Pray together for special people in your lives.

48. Call ahead, then take a tour of the local fire station.

49. Blow bubbles in the backyard.

50. At Christmas, Easter, Independence Day, or some other special occasion, put on plays with your children to dramatize the meaning of the holiday.

51. For each child's twelfth birthday, give him a jar with fifty-two "Special Treat" slips. Your child can draw one slip per week. Include simple treats as well as more elaborate (for example, "Stay up an hour later one night this week," "Invite a friend to spend the night," "Go to an ice cream or yogurt shop with Dad").

52. Serve together in some community or church project. Serve food at a homeless shelter or volunteer to help in the church nursery.

53. Take community school classes together: photography, woodworking, basic auto mechanics or home repair, anything that interests you.

54. Write letters to shut-ins from your church, or visit local nursing homes with a puppy for the patients to cuddle.

55. Begin reading C. S. Lewis's *The Chronicles of Narnia* together.

56. Surprise your child by picking him up at school and taking him to a movie, on a picnic, or out for pizza.

57. Arrange to have lunch with your young child at school.

58. Plan a "Hidden Supper." Hide quick-fix items throughout the house, then give a clue to where the first item is located (the second clue is found with the first item, and so on). Fix the food items together.

59. Have an "Honor Night" for each family member. Prepare that person's favorite meal, have a special place of honor at the table, design an honor plaque, and have each family member share "What I appreciate about . . ."

60. Once a month, plan a formal dinner. Everyone dresses up and the table is spread with the fancy china. Use this fun occasion to teach etiquette.

ENDNOTES

CHAPTER 1: BEING A DAD IN TOUGH TIMES

1. Compiled from figures published by the Children's Defense Fund and the book *13th Generation* by Neil Howe and Bill Strauss, and a *Fortune* magazine special report, "Children in Crisis: The Struggle to Save American's Kids," August 10, 1992.
2. Louis O. Caldwell, *When Partners Become Parents* (Grand Rapids, MI: Baker Book House, n.d.)
3. Claudia Wallis, "Stress: Can We Cope?" *Time* (June 6, 1983), 48–54.
4. Kathleen Fury, "Sex and the American Teenager," *Ladies' Home Journal* (March 1986), 60.
5. Armand Nicholi, Jr, "Changes in the America Family," *White House Paper* (October 25, 1984), 7–8.
6. Josh McDowell and Bob Hostetler, *Right from Wrong*, (Dallas: Word Publishing, 1994), 255.

CHAPTER 3: THE FATHER'S UNCONDITIONAL LOVE AND ACCEPTANCE

1. Dan Benson, *The Total Man* (Wheaton, Ill.: Tyndale House Publishers, 1977), 26.

CHAPTER 4: THE FATHER'S PURITY

1. Jerry Adler, "Building a Better Dad," *Newsweek* (June 17, 1996), 61.
2. Kathleen Fury, "Sex and the American Teenager," *Ladies' Home Journal* (March 1986), 60.
3. Marilyn Elias, "Parents' Divorce Affects Sex Lives of Collegians," *USA Today* (November 8, 1989), 1D.
4. Christopher P. Andersen, *Father: The Figure and the Force* (New York: Warner Books, 1983), 86–87.
5. Frank Martin, *The Kid-Friendly Dad* (Downers Grove, IL: InterVarsity Press, 1994), 85.

6. Leslie Jane Nonkin, *I Wish My Parents Understood* (New York: Penguin Books, 1982), appendix 2, 58.

7. Reginald W. Bibby and Donald C. Posterski, *The Emerging Generation—An Inside Look at Canada's Teenagers* (Toronto: Irwin Publishing, 1985), 39.

8. Stewart Powell, "What Entertainers Are Doing to Our Kids," *U.S. News and World Report* (October 28, 1985), 46.

9. Carol Towarnicky, "Positive Images Needed to Combat Teenage Pregnancy," *Houston Chronicle* (January 12, 1986), 17–18.

10. As quoted in *Why Wait?* by Josh McDowell and Dick Day (San Bernardino, CA: Here's Life Publishers, 1987), 45.

11. Thomas L. Trevethan, *The Beauty of God's Holiness* (Downers Grove, IL: InterVarsity Press, 1995), 13.

12. Josh McDowell and Dick Day, *How to Be a Hero to Your Kids* (Dallas: Word Publishing, 1991), 132.

CHAPTER 5: THE FATHER'S TRUTH

1. "Top High School Students Admit They Have Cheated," Associated Press story appearing in the *Hamilton Journal-News* (October 20, 1993).

2. George Barna, *The Invisible Generation* (Glendale, CA: Barna Research Group, 1992), 81.

3. Dennis Rainey, *Pulling Weeds, Planting Seeds* (San Bernardino, CA: Here's Life Publishers, 1989), 29–30.

CHAPTER 6: THE TRUSTWORTHY FATHER

1. James L. Schaller, *The Search for Lost Fathering* (Grand Rapids, MI: Fleming H. Revell, 1995), 142–43. (NOTE: Gordon MacDonald, in his book, *The Effective Father*, attributes this story to the life of James Boswell, the famous biographer of Samuel Johnson, whose father was a distinguished judge.)

2. Two resources that would be helpful for a father who wishes to clearly define his promises to his children: *Tell Me the Promises*, Joni Eareckson Tada and Ron DiCianni (Wheaton, IL: Crossway Books, 1996), and *A Father's Covenant: 173 Promises for*

Consideration and Reflection, Stephen Gabriel (San Francisco: HarperSanFrancisco, 1996).

CHAPTER 7: THE FATHER WHO COMFORTS
AND SUPPORTS

1. Dr. David Ferguson and Dr. Don McMinn, *Top 10 Intimacy Needs* (Austin, TX: Intimacy Press, 1994), 52–53.
2. See Phillip Keller's classic, *A Shepherd Looks at Psalm 23* for further description of the shepherd's rod and staff (Grand Rapids, MI: Zondervan Publishing House, 1970).
3. Dan Benson, *The Total Man* (Wheaton, IL: Tyndale House Publishers, 1977), 183.

CHAPTER 8: THE FATHER AS REFUGE

1. Cited in "The Facts About Teen Suicide," by David Elkind, *Parents' Magazine* (January 1990), 111.
2. The 24th Annual Survey of High Achievers by *Who's Who Among American High School Students*, cited in "Top High School Students Admit They Have Cheated," *Hamilton Journal-News*, (October 20, 1993).
3. Nadine Brozan, "New Look at Fears of Children," *New York Times* (May 2, 1983), B5.

CHAPTER 9: THE FATHER AS FRIEND

1. Jerry Adler, "Building a Better Dad," *Newsweek* (June 17, 1996), 60.

CHAPTER 10: THE FATHER WHO DISCIPLINES

1. McDowell and Day, *How to Be a Hero to Your Kids*, 29.
2. John Rosemond, "Successful Discipline," *Better Homes and Gardens* (April 1994), 32.
3. Ibid.
4. McDowell and Day, *How to Be a Hero to Your Kids*, 199–200.
5. Ibid., 201.

CHAPTER 11: THE FATHER AND FORGIVENESS

1. Allen C. Guelzo, "Fear of Forgiving," *Christianity Today* (February 8, 1993), 42.
2. McDowell and Day, *How to Be a Hero to Your Kids*, 204.

CHAPTER 12: THE FATHER AND RESPECT

1. As quoted in *What They Did Right*, Virginia Hearn, ed. (Wheaton, IL: Tyndale House Publishers, 1974), 166–167.
2. Dr. James Dobson, *The Strong-Willed Child* (Wheaton, IL: Tyndale House Publishers), 132.

CHAPTER 13: A FATHER AFTER GOD'S OWN HEART

1. Jerry Adler, "Building a Better Dad," *Newsweek* (June 17, 1996), 59.
2. Myriam Weisang Misrach, "The Wicked Stepmother and Other Nasty Myths," *Redbook* (July 1993), 88.
3. http://www.successfulstepfamilies.com/view.php/id/24.

ACKNOWLEDGMENTS

I want to recognize an invaluable team of people who helped make this book a reality:

Norm Wakefield, who has had a profound influence on me as a father. His insights (in a book we wrote together entitled *The Dad Difference*) have greatly sharpened my view of the heavenly Father's role in my life as a father. Norm's deep commitment to live in the image of God is reflected in the many illustrations from his life which I have used in this book;

Larry Keefauver, for his help in developing the first draft of this manuscript;

Bob Hostetler, for his help in shaping and molding the first draft into its final form;

Janis Whipple of Broadman & Holman for her support and expertise in originally guiding this project through the editorial process; and Paul Mikos, Jeff Godby, and Lawrence Kimbrough for their work on this current edition;

Dave Bellis, my associate of many years, for brainstorming the outline, creatively structuring the book, and facilitating the entire project through the maze of details to completion;

And, finally, to my wife Dottie and my children, Sean, Kelly, Katie, and Heather, for their patience, love, and support, and for giving me on-the-job training in becoming a better father.

Josh McDowell